M000312425

CHRISTA JOHNSON, M.D.

Mama J Unchained

The Potential Joy and Freedom in Aging

Mama J Unchained

The Potential Joy and Freedom in Aging

print ISBN: 978-1-66789-488-1
ebook ISBN: 978-1-66789-489-8

Contents

The Potential Joy and Freedom of Aging

AS I HAVE BEEN TOO BUSY—HAVING FUN, MOSTLY—
this book has been languishing, fully outlined, for months on the back burner of the stove that is my life. Since proudly declaring on my birthday just four weeks ago that my seventies would be the best decade of my life, I have been traveling, exercising like a fiend, setting Herculean goals, and satisfying my lifelong wish to excel at everything, including aging. I have such gratitude for a personality that gives me no choice but to fully engage in life. I am grateful also for the lenses, albeit rose-colored, that allow me to see the best in even the most difficult situations.

I was just released from the hospital after sustaining a heart attack. One week ago, I suffered acute, severe shortness of breath and had to be jet skied out of Buzzards Bay, where I was doing a 1.2-mile swim challenge. Labs determined I was indeed in the middle of what might have been "the big one." When my Covid test came back positive, I was relieved that this heart issue may be Covid related and thus temporary. Covid myocarditis was the discharge diagnosis. Permanent heart damage (or not) will be determined by further outpatient cardiac studies. (The fact that Covid is a BEAST cannot be denied; however, that is a discussion for another place and time.)

Having allowed myself to have a tearful day yesterday, I grieved for what might be lost in all this. I grieved that my healthy swimming addiction might have to bow to the demands of an inflamed heart. I grieved that my Superwoman cape would need to be covered with mothballs for the time being. I grieved that my recent mastery over my physical conditioning and lifelong weight problem would take a huge step backward, never to rebound.

Well, that was yesterday. Upon awakening this morning, I recognized the hand of the cosmic universe sending me a not-so-subtle message. "Not so fast, Miss Zippy! How about using this time to reflect on your aging future more gently instead of negatively?"

Now that I am restricted from swimming my usual two hours a day, I have time to help this book crystalize. The heart issue will certainly help soften it and make it much more real. For that, I am grateful.

Realities

YOU WILL DIE. YOU WILL GET SICK. YOU WILL LOSE people you love. You will lose your prior abilities. Your memory will go. Your vision will get worse. Your hearing will become challenging. You will get aches and pains in places you never even knew existed. Weight loss is harder even as your appetite wanes. Physical activity is more challenging. Just taking in a full breath can feel impossible. The temptation to just sit at home, watch TV, and nap is ever present. These are all truths, many of which are unavoidable.

Acceptance of these realities is crucial, but what we need is healthy acceptance, not giving up. Healthy acceptance is not denial. It means doing everything you possibly can to make your last years joyful, despite it all. This requires looking at everything in a different way and not accepting the usual concept of the aging process.

Traditional views of aging miss the incredible gifts that come along with getting older. Recognizing and embracing these gifts is the secret to fully living right up to the end, not giving up two or three decades before it is necessary. That is what this book is about.

The good news is it is never too late to start. And because everyone will get here eventually, it is never too early either. In fact, healthy acceptance is absolutely required, even when we are young.

No one comes to old age unscathed. The cosmic universe sends us sucker punches on a regular basis that follow us throughout our lives. Successfully navigating the tough times, though incredibly painful, will give you gifts and knowledge (and yes, a few scars) to use for the rest of your life. This is not just "having a positive attitude." It takes a lot of work and introspection and is probably the most important and rewarding work you will do throughout your whole life. So, what do you say? Are you ready to dive into this newest chapter of your life with me?

Retirement

I HAD NO IDEA HOW I WOULD FEEL LEAVING THE home of the gentleman who would be the last patient of my career as a hospice and family physician. This fulfilling and heartfelt career was central to my identity as a human being. Would I be devastated or relieved? Would there be a few gentle tears or a forceful gnashing of teeth as my perceived usefulness in the world faded away? Would I miss the relationships forged every day with staff and patients with whom I shared and from whom I learned so much? Of course I would; how could I not?

Much to my surprise, I did not cry as I descended the steps of that home. I floated. The weight of the world that I willingly took onto my shoulders the minute I entered med school was lifted. I did not realize how intense it was until it was gone. Administrative tasks, endless meetings, and the disappearance of the kind of medicine I wanted to practice were mind- and soul-numbing. Arguments with higher-ups whose only concern was higher numbers will not be missed. I believe docs need at least a little time for the purpose of healing, not just curing the patient, but that's just me. The beings I was allowed to touch and who touched me are a part of me now; they will never disappear, and they provide the richest foundation on which to build whatever comes next. The crisp blue sky, the sparkling yet powerful sunshine, the richly colored gardens, and little children on bikes all accompanied me on my floating journey that day, which continues now seven years later.

How do you see your retirement? Something you have been working toward all your life? The rest and relaxation you never had time for before? Travel to other places on this incredibly beautiful planet? Sacred time spent with grandchildren? Just smelling the roses, man, how would that be? Forging new interests and precious new friendships for which you now have all the time in the world? Or do you see it as the death of your productivity—your usefulness in the world? Is your identity hopelessly attached to what you did in the world rather than who you are and what is now possible? Are you angry it all had to come to this?

So many questions, the answers to which make all the difference. In life and in retirement, it is very much about choice. We really do have choices, although it may not seem so during "down" periods of our lives, of which there are many.

Okay, Ms. Rose-Colored Glasses, what if you are poor? What if you are sick? What if floating is just new age pablum you are trying to shove down our throats?

Touché!

Life can and does really suck at times. This is reality, for everyone, at one time or another. There is no whitewashing it. But there are still choices to be made. Love or hate, acceptance or bold rejection, peace or turmoil, trying or giving up, going with the flow or fighting to the death—these are all choices. Choose wisely—your peace and happiness depend on it, no matter what is going on.

Ahh, but I Was Such a Beauty

I NEVER SAW MYSELF THAT WAY; THEREFORE, THE loss of physical beauty is something I do not have to grieve. I must say, I really love my wrinkles, every one, well-earned and rich in character. I now have the lightest of blond hair (okay, it's white) that I spent hours as a teen trying to achieve with lemon juice! Having never been thin a day in my life, the loss of a gorgeous, slim and desirable body (at least according to present-day standards) is no biggie.

Looking back at pictures, I wasn't half bad, really, in retrospect. But we, especially women, are brutal to ourselves, never skinny or beautiful enough. How much time have you wasted berating yourself when you have most likely been quite beautiful all along? Way too much, in my case.

The havoc aging will wreak on our physical appearance is undeniable. Wrinkles, gray or balding heads, paunchy beer bellies, and post-baby guts will further deteriorate with the help of gravity. Same goes for boobs, dark circles under the eyes, and flabby upper arms. No matter how much exercise you do, veiny legs, old-age spots, and rear-end spread are inevitable. This is only a partial list of all the wondrous possibilities. What is to be done about this? Where are the CHOICES here?

Well, there are always choices. Plastic surgery is an option, and one that should not be dismissed if that is important to you. If it makes you feel better about yourself, then go for it. Just don't question your value as a person either way.

Ram Dass, in his beautiful book on aging, *Still Here*, says doing things to try to look young despite advancing years is kind of like painting all the leaves on a tree green. It makes summer appear to last longer but fall and winter will come. Green paint will also cover up the incredible reds, golds, and oranges that grace us in the fall. And there is just no stopping those leaves from getting crunchy brown and falling, as we all will.

Another good choice is exercise. As mother, wife, doctor, lecturer, writer, soccer manager, backstage mama, overachiever, I never had time to exercise! Sound familiar? This suggestion always pissed me off, frankly. How dare anyone suggest I must drag myself off to the gym too?

So here I am, retired. No more excuses. I can no longer let fear of pain, sweat, shortness of breath or being seen in spandex or a swimsuit stop me. I also have a particularly beautiful and fit group of friends, admittedly a little younger than me (the GWA, Girls' Week Away, as we are known) encouraging me along the way, without judgment.

So off I went to Round Hill Beach to swim. Endorphins kicked in immediately and it was no time at all before I was swimming a mile or two a day. Pounds came off, everything started to look better and, most important, I never felt better, NEVER! I never looked back. My recent heart attack has given me pause, for sure. But I will get back. I need to.

One more little tidbit—I understand that a well-positioned pair of Spanx can make a slight difference without any harm! Just this minute, I got my first pair delivered by the UPS guy. I will let you know how it works out.

A Gift from Facebook, of All Places

WHILE I WAS SITTING IN MY HOSPITAL BED LAST WEEK, Facebook gifted me with the most beautiful words ever written about this subject by Dame Judi Dench.

> Don't prioritize your looks my friend, as they won't last the journey.
> Your sense of humour though, will only get better with age.
> Your intuition will grow and expand like a majestic cloak of wisdom.
> Your ability to choose your battles, will be fine-tuned to perfection.
> Your capacity for stillness, for living in the moment, will blossom.
> Your desire to live each and every moment will transcend all other wants.
> Your instinct for knowing what (and who) is worth your time, will grow and
> flourish like ivy on a castle wall.
> Don't prioritize your looks my friend, they will change forevermore, that pursuit
> is one of much sadness and disappointment.

Prioritize the uniqueness that makes you, you, and the invisible magnet that draws in other like-minded souls to dance in your orbit.

These are the things which will only get better.

So, Who Is This Mama J?

A NAME GIVEN TO ME BY MY DAUGHTER'S FRIEND Hilary and adopted by several my children's friends, Mama J epitomized the essence of motherhood to me. All parents look back (mostly) fondly on the years we spent raising our children. If we are lucky, the good times far outweigh the bad.

How we preserve these memories is a choice. Focusing on the gurgling, toothless smiles of our baby rather than the endless, sleepless nights and the often-futile attempts to soothe him or her is a choice. Remembering childbirth as an incredibly miraculous experience rather than "I almost died giving birth to you after twenty-three hours of labor" (yeah, that was my mother's birthday greeting each and every year) is a choice. I adopted my children, so I have no real skin in this particular game.

I always wanted to have the fun house on the street. Having a pool helped! Kids, dogs, noise, hundreds of wet towels, pure chaos (did I mention noise?). This was motherhood at its best. One evening my husband came home as I was feeding dinner to five children.

"Well, Christa," he said, "this is all very nice, but none of these children are ours!"

That was the nature of the perfect neighborhood, in my estimation, as our kids were happily munching away at one of my neighbors' houses.

Total engagement in our children's lives, not only when they are babies, but later in sports, dance and myriad other activities changes our lives. But what happens when this much-loved vibrant life comes to an end? The tight and necessary "chains" that keep us a loving family will someday need to loosen and break so kids can become the adults they are meant to be. And boy, do they help in this regard! The "I love you, Mommies" and the snuggles steadily decrease. Not only are we no longer heroes to our kids, but instead we are something to be ashamed of. How ridiculously stupid we parents suddenly all became. Can't you just hear those chains snapping, link by link?

This is one of the most painful transitions we must endure. Even after living with this reality for decades, don't most of us yearn to return to this sweet family bubble every so often? And yet to loosen and break is the natural and healthy destiny of these chains.

And choices? Again, they abound. Sure, becoming depressed, whiny, needy and demanding our children still bow to our needs is a possibility (an ugly one, but a possibility nonetheless), guaranteed to ruin the lives of everyone involved. Yet this happens sometimes, does it not? This can be the stepping-off point for decades of giving up on life before it's necessary.

Another option is to grieve and recognize the reality of this sadness but to start working diligently on other valuable contributions you can give to the world, or JUST HAVE SOME FUN, for God's sake! We will probably have five or six decades after the kids are gone. Wasting them moaning should NOT be an option. So, Mama J is indeed unchained and the options that lie ahead are breathtaking.

Oh, and I still do love my children more than life itself.

Sweetie, Honey

A COMPLAINT OFTEN REGISTERED BY ELDERS IS THAT it is insulting to be arbitrarily dismissed by younger people as somehow less than. When I started being called sweetie, honey and the like by waitresses, store clerks, youths of all description, I recognized, "Yep, it's happening to me." But being insulted just wasn't my reaction. I found it quite endearing. They could have been calling me an asshole, a stupid old fool or much worse.

Honey and sweetie have a softness to them that makes me feel all warm and fuzzy inside. Sure, it is a recognition that I am older, but that is a reality with which I am at peace. Being at peace with getting older is the key to making it not only just all right but quite wonderful. This also gives me license to call everybody else sweetie and honey as name recall is no longer my strong suit. Kind of a win-win, as I see it.

On one occasion, I was dancing to music being performed by a dear friend's band. A cute, twentysomething woman came over after, placed her hand on my arm and said, "You go, girl." At sixty or so, I didn't feel that ancient, but it is all in the eye of the beholder, isn't it? Instead of my being insulted, this resulted in gales of laughter between my friend Laurie and me, a memory of joy not to be forgotten.

Thank You, Officer Hobbs

A FEW YEARS BACK, I WAS HEADING HOME FROM one of my joyful trips to Provincetown. This very beautiful, magical tip of Cape Cod has always been a place where I felt welcomed and cared for, a place where everyone is accepted as they are, without judgment. At eighteen or at seventy, I can step into a bar or restaurant and leave with hugs and a brand-new bunch of dear friends—special indeed. To walk along the shores of the unspoiled Cape Cod National Seashore is transformational at every level. It quite literally makes my inner being sing!

There is a section of Route 6 in Truro where the speed limit drops precipitously from 55 to 30 with no warning or necessity as I see it. Bebopping along at 60 miles per hour, I see those ominous blue lights pulling up behind me. With license and registration in hand, I had my first meeting with Officer Hobbs. My childhood friend Jan Hobbs had a place in Truro for many years, so the conversation about their possible common roots ensued. No relation, as it turns out.

Nudged by the officer back to the speeding issue, I was still smiling and engaging as I do in P-town bars, hoping, I guess, to have found yet another friend. His response was not a hug but not a ticket either. He said, "Mrs. Johnson, I really care about you and just want to make sure that you remain safe. Please slow down." Sounds like a new friend to me!!

A few years later, in the very same area, Officer Hobbs and I had our second meeting. "Officer Hobbs!" I said with great enthusiasm.

Seeing my license, he said in his best Eeyore voice, "Oh, hello, Mrs. Johnson."

I raised the volume of my radio to point out that, I kid you not, the oldie but goodie song "Little old lady from Pasadena" (old person's reference: a song from the sixties by the Beach Boys about a cool, drag racing old lady) was playing at just that moment. With a little smirk and a shake of his head, he just walked away, realizing getting serious with me was most likely for naught.

Now, do you think any of this would have happened when I was a youngster? Doubtful. Back in the day, I suppose, showing a little leg might have helped. This probably wouldn't have had the same effect at seventy. A little chuckle was the best I could hope for. But a sweet, smiley, white-haired, little old lady still holds some sway. Use what you've got.

Nothing to Prove

IT IS A GLORIOUS DAY INDEED WHEN WE CAN LET GO of the need to "succeed" or impress people with our accomplishments. An overachiever from birth, I pressured myself day in and day out to be perfect; anything short of that was failure. Saving the world was my goal, a ludicrous aspiration in retrospect.

Don't get me wrong, working hard and lofty goals keep this world functioning at its best, but they also put a great deal of pressure on those of us who take it to an extreme. Letting go of this pressure is not an overnight process. But as we let a few rays of light in between the hours of overworked insanity, other possibilities appear. We may discover, perhaps, we are good enough just as we are. Perhaps our smiles and sense of well-being affect the world as positively as being the best achiever who ever lived. Perhaps the greatest gift we can give to the world is to just be present.

The simplicity of offering a shoulder to someone who may be having a tough time or having an uproarious good time with old friends and new is more than adequate. Perhaps it's not the Hokey Pokey but quality time playing with your grandchild that is truly what it is all about. Kind of makes getting older rather appealing, don't you think?

Meanwhile, please ignore that crazy woman who is swimming miles and miles every day at seventy. Apparently, this perfection thing does not depart without a fight. I pray this recent heart attack will not take swimming away from me. But, for the moment, bowing to the needs of being seventy isn't entirely a bad thing. Yet another work in progress.

Lens Replacements

YES, SQUINTING UNSUCCESSFULLY TO DECIPHER
menus, unable to see big green highway signs and becoming a menace
on the roads was certainly part of my pre-cataract surgery life, but
these are not the lenses about which I am speaking.

What do we do with the memories of the bad times in our lives?
Memories alone have the potential to strip us of so much of the joy life
has to offer. Thankfully, I chose to talk to both therapists and friends
about having had an alcoholic, abusive mother and an ex-husband
who just announced one day he didn't want to be married anymore;
that I suffered from infertility and that my beautiful adopted child
was diagnosed with Tourette's syndrome; that my best friend died of
ovarian cancer at thirty-five, my dearest med school friend died of
stomach cancer at thirty, and my current husband had a stroke at age
fifty-four, requiring full-time care for the rest of his life.

This is a partial list. I do not know anyone for whom the list is
shorter or easier. Time for processing and grieving all the losses in our
lives is crucial to functioning at all ever again. But the real challenge in
all of this is figuring out how to move on, how to thrive despite all the
forces that can and do knock us for a loop, time and time again. How
many psychology textbooks well-trained therapists, clergymen, pop
psychology experts, etc. etc. have been trying to explain this since the

beginning of time? Taking a deep breath, I will, with great humility, take a whack at it. Becoming a Pollyanna here would be too easy. It would also make me gag.

Life Is Hard

ACCORDING TO BUDDHIST PHILOSOPHY, LIFE IS SUF-
fering. What the hell kind of philosophy is that? In modern Western culture, we are taught to believe that normal is being healthy, having romantic and sexy relationships that last unchanged forever and having perfectly behaved children (and parents). Success, if you work hard enough for it, is available to everyone. Having a house with a white picket fence is setting a low bar when mini-mansions, yachts and 24K gold toilets are available.

These unrealistic expectations come at a huge cost—the anger that ensues when these "rights" are not available to us. Perhaps even more devastating is achieving some of these goals then realizing they won't provide the kind of happiness and fulfillment we are really seeking. We blame our imperfect parents, we are disappointed in our difficult teenagers, we hate ourselves for being fat, or stupid or lazy. We rage at doctors who may not be able to make us well and sue them too, God damn it!

We don't suffer because we don't have everything we want; it is our expectation that life is supposed to be perfect and that everything is our birthright that gets us in trouble. We're never satisfied because there is always more out there that we so richly deserve. Buddhists refer to this phenomenon as the hungry ghost. Hungry ghosts are beings with huge appetites who have tiny throats, so they are never able to get all the nourishment they deserve. Like the hungry ghosts, we struggle with never having or being enough. We have difficulty making peace with our reality, whatever it is, at any given moment.

Accepting Difficult Realities

WHEN MY FRIEND BETH WAS IN THE HOSPITAL JUST prior to her death from stomach cancer, we heard a gentleman across the hall screaming, "Why me? Why me? It's not fair!"

He had temporary paralysis from Guillain-Barre syndrome, which would gradually, with support, resolve on its own. With all due respect for this man's suffering, which was overwhelming, I couldn't help but be pissed off at him as my dear friend was passing right before my eyes. In her last days, she was much kinder in her assessment of him than I. She told me she felt so sorry for him because he just didn't get that fairness has absolutely nothing to do with life. Her response instead was, "Why not me?"

Despite what we have been told, fairness has nothing whatsoever to do with human reality. Shit happens, all the time. What a blessing it would be if we could all take it like my friend Beth who in her final days totally got it.

Silver Linings

THIS IS A POLLYANNAISH CONCEPT IF I EVER HEARD one, but not so fast! Can anyone deny that the most significant growth periods of our lives happen in response to the times when we are the most hurt, anguished and afraid? When life falls apart, we are broken into little pieces. It is that very breaking that allows new light to enter and show us a different perspective. The work we must do to see our way through does in fact make us better, stronger, more compassionate and a little more equipped to deal with the next trauma.

Sitting by the campus pond at UMass after my first husband made his abrupt departure, I experienced something I will never forget. Through a profusion of tears, suddenly the world was more beautiful than I had ever seen it. The cherry blossoms were radiant as the sun kissed their branches. The grass was never greener. The dragonflies skimming the surface of the pond delighted me. The fluffy clouds floating above seemed to promise me softness and freedom if only I could embrace them in all their meaning. The opaque bubble of horror and fear I had built around my sadness and disappointment shattered in that one moment of grace. In that moment, I knew I would be okay.

So, when the darkness of aging and all the scary stuff that comes along with it surrounds you, as it will, just be with it, see it, experience it, cry as long and as hard as you need to, but let the rays of light in.

Allow the beauty of the moon rising over the water, the laughter of a small child or the smile from someone you love break through, just a little. In time, everything will change.

I am not asking you to rewrite history. I am not asking that you pick yourself up by your bootstraps, put on a happy face and just get over it. I am not saying that all you need is a positive attitude (please shoot me if I ever do). What I am saying is that experiencing life's horrible times as well as the glorious ones can allow you to see your world with more mature, softer lenses. Go ahead, visit some of those bad old days, but do so with the new lenses of maturity, experience and compassion. Everything changes without rewriting a single word of history.

You Must Be Yourself

SO CONCERNED WITH HOW WE APPEAR TO THE world, many of us were self-conscious for so much of our lives. Afraid to be seen as weird, gay, too smart (a brain), too stupid (a moron) or weak (a loser), we stopped being fully who we are. What a tragedy! Women are particularly chameleonlike and tend to become more like their spouses, or their bosses, even their children, so insecure that who they really are is just not good enough. Or, even worse, they keep themselves down so as not to make anyone feel bad or less than in some way.

The culture of male dominance is alive and well. Certainly, in my generation, girls were taught they shouldn't be too smart, too strong, too educated or too ambitious as this would make prospective male mates run in the other direction or, even worse, make them feel bad. Though much more subtle than it was in my day, that message persists for girls/women.

I tried extremely hard to be more "doctor like," stern, serious, with all the gravitas of that profession, not always successfully. My real self was way more Patch Adams (old person reference: a very unconventional doctor portrayed by Robin Williams who recognized that traditional medicine treats only a small part of who the person is) than Dr. House (a genius diagnostician without a drop of humanity).

Attempts to keep that under wraps were detrimental to me personally and, I fear, to patients who may well have benefited more from who I really was as a doctor. Luckily, Patch was always there inside me somewhere, smirking and winking at patients as the loftier of the MD breed passed by. I was very much the proverbial square peg attempting to stuff myself into the round hole of traditional medicine. It was torture!

Speaking of being a square peg, everyone in my immediate family is shy, not very sociable—then there is me. Keeping a whirlwind in a box is not likely to be successful. But, God knows, I tried. But, Halleluiah, praise the Lord, there will be no more of that! With nothing else to prove and no one I feel obligated to please, this is a whole new ball game. Let the fun begin!

Dancing Queen

THERE IS NOTHING MORE ENERGIZING AND LIFE affirming than doing things you have been afraid to do in the past. Insecure about my body, or God knows what, I would dance only under duress. God forbid I should expose myself to looking silly. Now, dancing whenever I hear music at home, parties, the grocery store, Sears Auto Parts, I just have fun! (You go girl, indeed.) Instead of weird looks, I get mostly oh-isn't-she-adorable looks (the sweet little old lady effect). I am definitely okay with that. But then again, even if they are weird looks, my new and improved lenses do not see it that way.

Stepping Out of Your Comfort Zone

WEARING SWIMSUITS, SPANDEX OR DRESSES IN younger years was very daunting, the tyranny of not being perfect hanging precipitously overhead. My aforementioned GWA girls always look so cute in their dresses and swimsuits, why shouldn't I? True, I have lost some weight, but I no longer see my body as imperfect, just real. Wow, what a freeing revelation that is for anyone, but especially for someone who is now seventy.

- Doing a polar plunge in Provincetown on New Year's Day… check.
- Traveling the world all by myself…double check (and fabulous, by the way).
- Walking over canyons on small suspension bridges, I'm game.
- Karaoke, never in my wildest dreams then, but now, bring it on.
- Any interesting invitation to do anything new will be given the most serious and enthusiastic consideration, and I am so much better for it.

The bucket list expands daily.

Just Go for It

IS THERE ANYTHING YOU ALWAYS WANTED TO TRY but for one reason or another never did? Why is that? Have you admired others challenging themselves in sports or creative endeavors but would scoff at yourself for even thinking such a thing? It is time to stop that.

Adventures with Bubble Boy

I STARTED DRUMMING WHEN I WAS ABOUT SIXTY. What is it about banging on things with music that is so satisfying? Steve, my drum instructor who is about my age, is now pursuing his drumming career in Austin, Texas. God bless him, he tried to teach me the right way, but one little tap at a time was frustrating as I thought it would be more fun to become Alex Van Halen or Ringo Starr immediately. I am kind of shocked really that I have yet to be pulled over for drumming and dancing while driving. Oh, Officer Hobbs, have you taught me nothing? I no longer have any restraint when music enters my consciousness.

Steve is a serious marijuana user. He has a machine called the Volcano that vaporizes marijuana in this big bubble. Having never had much experience with this sort of thing, I had a few hits at each lesson. I cannot say I liked it much. It made me dizzy, but the experience of doing something a little naughty and so unlike me was liberating. The fact that I am a crappy drummer does not stop my fantasy of playing "Wipe Out" publicly for my eightieth birthday.

One must have goals, if for no other reason than keeping oneself upright and moving forward. The actual outcome is irrelevant.

The Value of the Bucket List

FEEL FREE TO BE OUTRAGEOUS NOW. WHAT NEW experience would you find liberating? Scuba diving? Swimming or diving lessons? Whitewater rafting? Voice lessons? Paragliding? Something more sedate, perhaps? Painting, writing poetry or that book that has always been in the back of your mind? The sky is the limit! Nothing is impossible (well, maybe a few things). The only error you can make is not putting yourself out there, not trying. You have nothing to lose, but ever so much to gain.

Travel is the most precious of bucket list items. If you have resources, travel can be the most mind-expanding, eye-opening experience imaginable. It is not just the amazing places you see; it is the people! There is no better way to change or improve your perspective than by opening yourself up to people from other cultures, other races, other sexual orientations, just other, period. World peace will never be possible until we open ourselves to everyone in this way. Heck, you don't even need to travel. It is opening to and accepting others just as they are that makes all the difference in yourself and the world.

Shenanigans

I HAVE NEVER BEEN MUCH OF A DRINKER OR IMBIBER of substances of any kind. Having seen what alcohol has done to family members, friends and everyone who loves them, being a teetotaler was my only viable option for many years.

That was then, this is now.

I tease my friend Jack, who started inviting me out for cocktails during the thirteen years I was taking care of my very stroke-handicapped husband at home. Jack is responsible for putting me on this road to perdition! In truth, he and his shenanigans have been a lifesaver for me, for which I am forever grateful. Several other friends have also encouraged me along these same lines, but it is fun to give Jack crap about it. I now allow myself a drink or two with friends whenever we go out, and I discovered the best sushi bar near my house, where I go after my daily swim for a gin and tonic, lovely fresh sushi and the companionship of kind bartenders and other oldies but goodies like me hanging out in a bar at 4 p.m. Moderation in all things (except fun).

Old Friends, Not Bookends

SIMON AND GARFUNKEL WERE CLEARLY VERY young when they wrote "Bookends". This very sweet but depressing song portrays two old friends sitting on a park bench blathering away incoherently as if this is our only destiny upon reaching seventy; creased black -and-whites being all that remains of what barely even seems like a life anymore.

It is a sweet little song, but total NONSENSE! I am blessed to have so many friends from every decade of my life. I couldn't for one minute deny that it is because of them I am still here, in one piece. This is not hyperbole (I love that word!). This is my most dear truth. Each and every one, so special, fills a place in me no one else could.

But old friends contribute a whole new dimension to this discussion. The much-maligned Facebook has brought so many of these amazing people back into my life. Being with childhood friends adds another dimension to the joy of friendship. Remember the old days when you just laughed fitfully for hours and hours about the most ridiculous things? When the worries of adulthood weren't even a thought? When playing at recess, or exchanging notes in class, or talking about how handsome that Larry was (sorry, Larry, couldn't resist) was what life was all about?

It's a funny thing. Whenever I get together with these blasts from my past, laughter is uproarious anew. For a few moments in time, we're all back there, whooping it up. Our roots continue to be intertwined, in a way making them more like family. These old friends figure in a big way to the shenanigans of which I speak so fondly. Do not miss the opportunity to remember and welcome your old friends back into your life. This is one of the best gifts you could ever give to yourself and to each other!

You Did What?

IF YOU DON'T GET SEVERAL EYE ROLLS WHILE SHAR-ing stories of your senior shenanigans with your kids, you're not trying hard enough. When you have been the rule maker for so long, it comes as quite a shock when your kids must deal with you breaking the rules.

I took my oldest daughter and her boyfriend to my beloved P-town. You should have seen the look on their faces when one of my favorite bartenders came running out of his establishment to welcome me and give me a big hug. With wide eyes, Anna asked me if I was living a double life. I could not stop laughing! A double life? No, just a much expanded, truer one.

Unchained by all the choices I made to raise kids, have a demanding career and, yes, to be perfect, I am now free to experience my true potential on every level. How awesome is that?

Bitch, Bitch, Bitch

I MUST SHARE THIS LITTLE DITTY JUST SENT TO ME
from my old friend (definitely not bookend) Linda.

> I will bitch about heat I will bitch about cold.
> I will bitch about sunshine I will bitch about growing old.
> I will bitch about everything inside and out.
> You will find there is nothing I can't bitch about.
> (From Irish facts and funny stuff.)

We all know people like this. Sometimes it is even us doing the bitching. Bitching about stuff is not altogether a bad thing; however, less is definitely more. We have all been in the presence of people who whine about every pain, the people who displease them or how unfair life is, while lifting a shirt and showing you a particularly disturbing rash. (As a doc, you have no idea how much gross stuff I have been shown during an innocent conversation.) People like this give us old folks a really bad name!

We listen, using up very quickly any compassion we may have stored away. And then ask ourselves, *Is 10 a.m. too early for sushi and a gin and tonic?* God knows we all have a great deal about which to bitch, but why do it? This helps neither the bitcher nor the bitchee. God knows I could milk my recent heart attack for months to come, but what fun is that for me or for anyone who feels obliged to listen?

Sure, there are many times in our lives when we can't survive if we don't have dear friends willing to be with us through it all no matter how painful. They are without a doubt the most precious gifts in our lives. (You all know who you are, and I love you.) But allowing the pain and suffering to take over all the amazing possibilities of your life is the real sin, one that promises to deprive you of all that life can be.

The Fall and Rise of Jamaica Dane

YESTERDAY, HAVING FINISHED MY WRITING FOR THE day, I stopped for gas. I got into a conversation with the gas station owner about life, as I often do. He was there with his best friend from college after years of not having seen one another. This brought up the subject of old friends, which brought up my recent writing on the topic, which brought up the book he wants to write.

He is an immigrant from Jamaica. His story sounds terrifying but victorious at the end. Hence the title, first the fall, then the rise. I was so taken by this story and will now only get gas at his station so we can talk further.

It reminded me of how important it is to tell our stories for ourselves, for the world. Because I am an author of sorts, people always tell me about the books they would like to write. So, they should!! I think we get our knickers all in a twist about the outcome of our book being published, whether it will become a bestseller and whether it will make us rich. The fact that these things are unlikely to happen tends to stop us in our tracks. However, that says nothing about the brilliance or the value of the work.

Each story or thought is precious, both to the author and to everyone with whom the author shares it. I have no idea at this point whether this book will ever be published. But unlike when writing past books, I have no investment in any particular outcome. The writing and the sharing with anyone who may benefit from or just enjoy it is absolutely enough. It does not matter whether writing is an exercise in catharsis or just a way to give thoughts and stories concrete expression. It is the stories and their telling that matters.

What a gift it would be to sit with someone who is elderly, ill or even facing death and give them the time to tell their story, then write it down and privately publish a little book for them and their loved ones.

I just found the perfect volunteer work for myself.

Your story matters.

You matter.

You always will.

Still Woman, Still Roaring

COMING OF AGE IN THE LATE SIXTIES AND SEVENTIES, I embraced my hippiedom, much to the horror of my parents' generation. Wearing my George McGovern for President button and going to peace protests during my lunch hour while working at my first grown-up job as assistant stock trader at Fidelity funds (talk about irony), was of great concern to the happy capitalists with whom I worked. This was not destined to be my life's work.

Despite that bizarre blip, I am very proud to this day to be just an old hippy—not the sex, drugs and rock and roll kind, but the peace-loving, flower-presenting, civil rights-embracing kind. A snowflake, I guess, in current jargon. Undoubtedly naive, we all felt the possibility of a world at peace, a world where everybody was accepted, applauded for being just who they are, nothing more, nothing less.

Now, fifty years later, the sweetness of that naivety is but the slightest wisp of a memory. We have descended into a kind of hell where the needs of the self reign. The current concern for the common good is a sign of the evil of advancing socialism. Instead of giving people a hand up, we step on them, fearing their advance will somehow mean our decline. The zero-sum game appears to be the only one in town.

I wish I could say what could be done about all this. Having now gone back sixty years, to when "America was Great," I no longer have much hope that anything will significantly change in my lifetime. Recent Supreme Court decisions show, rather, that many desire going back to the fifties. This should not stop me or anyone else with a like mind to do what little we can. Whether it is wearing your "Power to the People" arm band to protests, or writing to your congressmen, or draping the Ukrainian flag lovingly around your home or just being kind to anyone who needs it, what remains is giving your love, generously, in one way or another. Millions of us old people have the time to do just this. Naive, perhaps, but powerful, nonetheless.

Power to the people!

Where Everybody Knows Your Name

WE ALL FONDLY REMEMBER WATCHING THE CUS-tomers of Cheers each week as their lives unfolded in that very special bar. As you have seen, I write about bars frequently. Perhaps assuming I am a total lush, you may be surprised to learn it is not the alcohol, but the people that beckons me. Carefully chosen bars provide the perfect atmosphere for just hanging out and meeting new people. Becoming a regular at a diner or some other gathering place is another happy option.

As a woman alone, societal expectation is we probably shouldn't hang out at bars by ourselves; most women still go along with this unwritten rule. I have my first husband to thank as his leaving left me partner-less, forcing me to just go for it. Assuming at twenty-three that no one would ever love me again, I needed to find a way to enjoy every single part of my life without the protection of a partner. He is still my friend to this day, and I thank him for giving me this incredible gift.

So now, some fifty years later, I am very experienced and very happy to venture anywhere in the world by myself, and what an incredible treat that is. Without someone else to hide behind, I am much more open to those around me, and this has opened a whole new world.

You may ask what this has to do with aging. Well, one of the indicators of healthy aging is continued engagement with the world. Perhaps widowed or alone for any number of reasons, people tend to shut themselves in, shutting everyone else out. This sets an aging person up for great sadness, depression and withdrawal, which in turn sets them up for more illness, pain and a dramatically shortened life.

I'm not saying everyone should hang out in bars or restaurants. I'm saying that staying engaged with the rest of humanity gives us the best shot at a longer, more fun, fulfilling and healthy life. A big, joyful engaged family goes a long way in this regard. Having dear friends is just what the doctor ordered for health and happiness for as long as we are around. But having a few places where everybody knows your name is a very special, life-affirming treat. I recommend you give it a try.

Antigua, My Home away from Home

LAST JANUARY, FATIGUED WITH THE COVID EPIDEMIC as we all were, I decided to take myself to someplace warm and sunny. Nothing like the Caribbean to soothe an aching soul. Randomly pouring over the Internet, I found a little condo complex right on Dickenson Bay, Antigua, that piqued my interest, so I booked it.

Having no expectation other than enjoying the warmth and sun and swimming for miles and miles in the sparkling turquoise water, I checked in. The first night, I floated around a bit and strolled on powdery white sand feeling ever so grateful for this miracle that we call the Caribbean and my solitude.

The next day, I started my daily swimming safaris. Swimming one half mile down the beach and stopping for breakfast or going another mile in the other direction to have jerk chicken prepared by locals on the beach was amazing. Nobody cared that this seventy-year-old lady came dripping, wearing nothing but a swimsuit and goggles, into their establishments, although many did comment that my daily escapades were pretty cool for a sweet old white-haired lady.

Everything changed when I swam up to the locally owned and operated Kon Tiki Bar and Grill. This floating tiki bar can be accessed only by boat or crazy swimmers like me. The fun-loving bartender and owner, Emma, slammed a rum punch down on the bar. Noticing my age and unusual swimming endurance, I suppose, she announced my money would be no good there. Thus began the party of my life.

This place, much like many of my haunts in P-town, was welcoming. Enjoyed by locals and more adventurous tourists alike, it is a place so small and fun that you become fast friends with everyone who happens to climb aboard.

I spent the first afternoon with an Irish flight crew from Virgin Atlantic Airlines. They were such gorgeous and fun young people, complete with Irish brogue and sense of humor. I was transfixed by them and them by me. Apparently, an old lady long-distance swimmer is not something you run into every day. It kind of reminded me of the pubs in Ireland where, while sipping on your Guinness, you attach immediately to the fun, kindness, gentleness, warmth, generosity, humor and spirit of these incredible people.

As the days unfolded, I met lots of Brits, some people from the United States, folks from other Caribbean and European countries, and on and on. I especially loved meeting the locals there. Having exposure to their culture, race and values, I was in pig heaven. Needless to say, I spent every afternoon thereafter welcoming everybody on board and hugging them when they left, usually closing the place every day. I went back five months later to celebrate my seventieth birthday, making more local friends and meeting other travelers every day, the perfect celebration. So to this magical place, where everyone is certainly getting to know my name, I will return as often and for as long as I can.

Channeling My Inner Patch Adams

MOST OF YOU PROBABLY REMEMBER THIS MOVIE, starring Robin Williams, about an unorthodox physician who felt, as I do, that being a doctor is a lot more than patching up bodies. Traditional practitioners, not inappropriately, see the human body as their only focus—diagnosing illness, treating it with meds or surgery and calling it a day. I don't for one minute demean what they do (I did) as unimportant by any stretch of the imagination. So much work, study, sleepless nights, worry, knowledge and expertise go into it, we can only stand back and marvel.

Having said that, Patch and I were acutely aware these bodies are just housing for something much more important. Like the mollusk, inside is where the action and life force lives. Without a functioning body, this precious, dare I say, inner being cannot survive. Traditional medicine is the best thing ever for curing the body, this miraculous, life-giving structure. But it is the recognition and respect for what lies within that allows for healing, not just curing.

You may remember Patch wearing his clown nose in pediatric wards, fulfilling an old lady's fantasy of swimming in a big pool of noodles and other healing shenanigans. I'm sure he also did all the crucial doctor things, as I did, but the warmth and love underlying all his silliness healed on the deepest of levels.

True, this may not be the doctor's job. But in caring for people, especially the elderly, this unorthodox approach can make all the difference. Whether it be doctors, nurses, aides, social workers or friends and family, the recognition and care of the person within the patient makes all the difference.

If You Want to Be Interesting, Stay Interested

A DEFINITE POTENTIAL PITFALL OF AGING IS THE TENdency to withdraw from the outside world. Yes, this is something we all need to do if we are dying, but, until that time, this tendency robs you yet again of so much that your life could be.

Younger people may need to limit time with anyone who becomes so boring and self-focused that it is a task to remain in their presence. What is to be done about this? Get yourself back into the ball game any way you can. Read, take lifelong education courses and just show up for your life and the people in it! Try focusing on the other person rather than yourself. I promise it will make you so much more interesting. And being interested makes your life more fun and rewarding. Work hard on this one.

When Our Kids Become Our Parents

THE DAY OUR KIDS MUST TAKE CARE OF US ON SOME level or another is a sad one for all involved. All parties are uncertain as to how to proceed with this role reversal, and there are often conflicts, mistakes are made, and it is horribly stressful. Unwittingly, while trying to keep the parent as safe and healthy as possible, kids become the rule makers and parents may feel resentful about their loss of control and not having a say any more about the life they want to live. Taking away a car is a perfect example.

In the ER, I used to have grown children dragging their elderly parents in, usually on a holiday as that is when family who don't see one another on a regular basis get together. Recognizing Mom or Dad isn't doing very well, they come to the doctor seeking support for some rule or restriction that wasn't sitting well with the parent. Complaining that Dad isn't sticking to his cardiac diet or that Mom still prefers to wash her own kitchen floor on hands and knees, they asked for my support. Unfortunately, I couldn't always give them what they wanted.

Well-intended restrictions must be considered very carefully. Just having been on a cardiac diet while hospitalized for my heart attack, I felt life may well not be worth living; I would have killed for a bag of Cape Cod chips! For God's sake, what is the harm in having a bit of restricted food when you're chronically ill and in your eighties?

The depression from yet another loss will kill your parent much sooner than one *malasada* (a delectable Portuguese fried dough) would. A compromise for the floor-cleaning situation may be making sure someone is around to assist the lady who is so passionate about her floor. No matter what, considering the being in the body rather than just the body is crucial to making every minute of our lives the best they can be. And that, my friends, is the goal.

Happiness or Contentment

AS WE AGE, THE OPPORTUNITIES FOR PARTICIPATING in what contributed to our "happiness" dwindle somewhat. The wild, hot romances, the adventurous excursions, the parties, the dynamic energy of buying a first home, getting engaged or having a baby are generally a thing of the past. Happiness, as we know it, is often situational and fleeting, leaving us aching for more.

A while back, my husband asked my son if he was happy. Mike didn't know how to answer immediately, recognizing that happiness is a temporary state—fun while it lasts, but not necessarily sustainable.

The better question, I thought, was "Are you content?" His yes response was immediate, given without a second thought. Contentment is more a state of being as opposed to a dependence upon the highs we so fervently seek. It is a baseline acceptance and appreciation of things just as they are.

The pursuit of "happiness" often involves grasping for the next rush, the next fun thing, a fancy new car, a vacation home, which may or may not ever come to pass. Even when they do, we are often dismayed that we are still not as happy as we deserve to be. Our expectation that those things will give us sustainable happiness sets us up again and again for disappointment.

Guillaume Apollinaire stated, "Now and then it's good to pause our search for happiness and just be happy."

I am more than willing to trade happiness for contentment every day of the week.

Worst Nightmare

MY KIND AND BRILLIANT HUSBAND HAD A DEVAStating stroke at age fifty-four. Also a doctor, he was a stroke specialist (irony much?) in charge of the rehab unit at my hospital. He was also the chief information officer in his spare time. With one fall in the night, I knew our lives were forever changed. Looking at his CT scan, I knew we weren't in Kansas anymore; we had descended into the depths of hell. He was an inpatient at hospitals and rehabs for six months.

This made me realize the truth that there is no shortcut through trauma and grief. For an unknown period, we must just go through it. Be angry, be sad, be hysterical, feel hopeless, sob, feel desperate. Did I mention sob? There is no way to escape it. Pulling yourself up by the bootstraps or forcing a positive attitude will join the trash heap of all the other things you tried and failed at in your life. Going through times like this, it is crucial to understand everything comes in its own time. The futility of forcing it is clear. Forcing it on yourself or having others force it on you is violence in its most basic form.

Unknowingly, people, in their attempt to help or comfort, say the most unhelpful things. "You just must have a positive attitude. Aren't you lucky he will be coming home? God never gives us more than we can handle. Just pull yourself up by your bootstraps and move along!" I almost decked my unsuspecting brother-in-law when he suggested I should just deal with my new normal! New normal indeed! It would take many months to years to sob enough, to look this monster in the face, to worry and plan and pray and grieve. Sure, a new normal would be necessary, just not yet please!!

It is beyond the scope of this book to get into what it is like taking care of someone who can in no way take care of himself in the home. Nor could I even pretend to be able to write cogently about what the past thirteen years have been like living his reality. Suffice it to say, it has been torture for all of us. I have overwhelming respect, love and empathy for all caregivers. They are without a doubt the living saints in this world.

That big, opaque dark bubble surrounded me again. I prayed for moments of grace like the one I had at UMass that would shatter this darkness as well. Slowly, but surely, they came.

Grace

WE ALL HAVE A VAGUE SENSE OF WHAT GRACE IS,
but it deserves some thought and clarification. It is something to which
we all have access, but, like a passing cloud, it is almost impossible
to grasp.

As I see it, grace is a moment in time when something so beautiful, so rich, so endearing overtakes our consciousness and changes
everything. For just a moment, it breaks through that prison that is
our ego and fractures it just enough that beautiful new light can filter
through, giving us a new perspective and peace.

My UMass experience was probably the first time I became
aware of the power of grace, although certainly it has been there from
the moment I first opened my eyes in this world.

Think back. Have you ever been so captivated by a piece of music
or a lyric that you could feel the tears well up from the pit of your
stomach? What happened when you got your first glimpse of your
new baby, or a new puppy, for that matter? Whether it was in labor
and delivery or at the Kennedy Airport where I picked up my little
ones arriving from Korea doesn't matter. It was magical, was it not?

Remembering my niece and nephew during one of our break-
fasts (okay, just donuts) at the beach many years ago, playing in the
sand, building castles, jumping around being superheroes always

brings me back to the warmth, fun and love of that moment. With my ego so bathed in light, it could do nothing but just stand back and admire. This moment of grace dissolved all other worries confronting me during that time of my life.

As I write this, I am sitting in my car overlooking the beach on an overcast day. I am so grateful for the small ocean waves trickling over the seaweed covered rocks returning from high tide to be warmed anew by the sandy beach it just left hours ago. Grace is everywhere. All we need to do is recognize it and be thankful. But during the chaos of our lives, moments of grace vanish before we are even aware of their presence. This happens all the time. How to capture these moments will be discussed at length in my meditation chapters to follow. But, for now, just ponder the possibilities.

Random episodes of grace are powerful indeed, but there is much more to it than that. We are given grace all the time by the people who love and care for us. The delivery of chicken soup by a friend when you have been ill, sharing a cup of coffee with someone who is so present, so dear as you go through yet another of life's struggles, contemplating the meaning of it all with a like-minded friend as you dig your toes in the warm sand on the beach. Moments of grace, given to you freely from those who love you are a treasure unlike any other.

What about all the times you have been the giver of grace? A gift for sure to the recipients of this act of love and caring, but even more so to yourself, the giver. I will always hold dear the moments I spent with my friend Lynn as she was gradually passing from this world to the next. I never appreciated the true sweetness of being totally present for the needs and desires of another person. She could no longer eat. She was uncomfortable. There didn't appear to be anything that anyone could do for her. I came to discover that sometimes doing nothing but being totally present is more than enough.

Just lying there together, feeling her gentle breathing beside me, nothing else mattered but this moment, this friend, and all we meant to one another. The words she spoke between her fitful naps were so precious, so brilliant coming from the place of knowing that I suspect only people who are near death can comprehend.

At one point she craved the taste of a spicy gumdrop. Off to the store I went. She couldn't swallow at this point, but the look on her face as she rolled this sweet morsel around her tongue was transporting. The fact that she needed to spit them out due to her inability to swallow didn't take away from the joy of that moment. Another day it was fried rice. She was very specific on this. It needed to come from a certain restaurant that used sesame oil to its best advantage. Again, the smile, the joy of remembering what a gift food was, was what she needed in that moment, what I needed in that moment.

As we age, retire and back away from all the demands of an ego trying desperately to make its place in the world, we have a beautiful opportunity to capture the grace that is there for the recognition. We have all the time in the world to accept grace given to us by others and to give them the grace of which we all have an endless supply.

There is a person right out in front of me bouncing joyfully through the waves. I can feel the perfection of joy, the fresh air, the salted breeze, the pleasant movement of the rolling waves beneath, the freedom and ecstasy I know he is feeling. His moment of grace is now mine, but I digress.

Moments of grace can be fleeting, but not always. There are times in our lives that everything just moves along swimmingly. Times when the kids are happy, work is going well, a vacation is just perfect, well-being abounds. Times when there is little effort, the winds and current guiding us to just where we should be. These times are not meant to last forever, but they do deserve enormous appreciation for as long as they do.

I know I'm in a grace period when I am writing. This is my fourth book. Not one of my books has been written through sheer force of will. They seem to just pop out of me when what needs to be said is so pressing that, in the moment, the stars and planets align, the wind, the currents just push me there, unbidden. What a gift. And one week after a heart attack, what great timing! As I said earlier, traumatic events do tend to break us open, the upside being a new awareness of the grace that is all around us.

Keepin' It Real

PERHAPS YOU'VE NOTICED HOW THIS BOOK bounces from sad to happy, joyous to challenging, funny to serious, and on and on. This mirrors our lives, does it not? From one moment to the next, we have no idea what will happen. But in Western culture, it better be good, God damn it, or somebody (even God himself) will be blamed.

The truth is blame is useless here. Life just happens. Beauty, wonder, joy, shit and sadness whirl all around us, 24/7/365, for as long as we live. Like the wheel of fortune, we have no idea where and when the wheel will stop.

Who Are You Really?

THIS QUESTION IS THE BASIS OF MUCH BUDDHIST inquiry. The usual answers to this question tend to be ego driven. Our careers, how we look, how amazing and brilliant our children are, our "successes" burst out in response to this very simple question. But is this who we really are? Buddhists believe, as do I, that these identities merely scratch the surface. Like the shell of a mollusk, we can be easily identified by our outside shell, but inside is where the action is.

Ego, Friend or Foe?

BEFORE I MAKE THE EGO THE VILLAIN IN ALL THIS, let's be clear. In order to function on this planet, we absolutely need our goal-driven egos to sustain our very lives. It is the ego that motivates us to work hard, take care of our families, put food on the table, get out of bed in the morning and attend to all the necessary, practical business of our lives. Period.

The counterpoint to our egos is something I refer to as inner being. Others may view this ego/inner being dichotomy instead as left brain/right brain or as sympathetic versus parasympathetic nervous system. I prefer the ego/inner being language as it includes the possibility of a spiritual side of our nature. The other terms suggest our bodies and minds are everything we are. This is how traditional medicine generally views it.

Finding ways to tap into our inner beings (right brain or parasympathetic nervous system if you prefer) is crucial for our health, happiness and inner peace. My beloved inner being plants me smack dab in the middle of my happy place. I spend a lot of time there, ask my friends! But thinking beautiful thoughts and basking in the reverie of the cosmic universe doesn't make the world go around, as it must. The ideal, as always, is balancing the two worlds.

But wait. How can we balance these worlds if the ego world is the only one with which we are familiar? We have all had glimpses of our inner being with brief blasts of peace, love, harmony and moments of grace. But what can we do to make it a more vibrant part of our lives? And how does this change everything?

Meditation

BEFORE YOUR EYES GLAZE OVER IN ANTICIPATION of some great mystical, otherworldly discussion of what meditation is all about, REJOICE! It is not that complicated. I will tell you what it really is and what it does without the expense of going to Nepal to follow some guru. Nothing against this, mind you, that is on my bucket list, but let's be real—most of us won't be traveling to India anytime soon.

Meditation is a way of training your mind to focus. Focus on what, you ask? Pretty much anything. In its simplest form, one can just focus on the breath. Attending to every detail and sensation of the breath going in and out is the best way to start. Many believe successful meditation involves a complete emptying of your mind (impossible) to bring you to some sort of nirvana. Except for mountain gurus, this is not the case. It is just an exercise to help put the mind (ego) at rest so what's inside (inner being) will be more able to express itself.

Why is this important? Well, in my estimation, this hidden, quiet part of our being is where all the good stuff is. The Buddhists refer to it as Buddha nature, the part of us that is naturally kind, loving, creative and intuitive. It is this silent part of us that needs to be accessed if the lofty goal of world peace or loving acceptance of "others" can ever happen. Some may prefer to call this a soul. That works for me as I believe it all comes down to the same thing.

Without the ego blocking the light, we can experience beauty and intelligence we don't even know we have. And despite how it may appear, especially these days, we ALL have Buddha nature. It's just more buried in some than others.

Just for yuks, stop for a minute, close your eyes and focus on your breath. As your mind wanders, which it will unmercifully, bring your attention back to the breath. Do it for just a few minutes.

The response to this tiny exercise varies from I felt totally relaxed, to I couldn't empty my mind, to I can't stay focused, to what the hell is this craziness supposed to do for me, to I just can't do this. I totally get it. But please consider the following.

Feeling relaxed is great. It is often a delightful side effect of meditation. But it is not the goal.

Emptying your mind? This will NEVER happen. Again, I leave this to the yogis who have been doing this for all their lives. They might have a shot at it for short periods of time. Again, this is not the goal.

I can't stay focused. Of course, you can't. Such is the nature of our ego-based consciousness. The ego will fight you every step of the way, fearing its importance will be lessened by inviting this inner being intruder in to play.

What is this supposed to do for me? So much can and will happen as a result of meditation, in time. The goal is simply to bring yourself back to focus time and time and time again. This keeps the ego at bay, just a little, to give your inner being a little space, a little breathing room, an invitation to matter and help you see life from a very different perspective.

What does meditation feel like? Well, picture yourself jumping around in the ocean with waves crashing overhead. Feel your body being tossed around uncontrollably and then take a big breath and sit yourself down for a moment about two feet or so beneath the surface. Suddenly, the chaos caused by the waves all around you is gone. It is very peaceful, silent and still, and you are totally present. Meditation takes you for periods of time away from the raging surf of your life. That's what it feels like.

And, finally, I can't do this. This is probably true if you have preconceived notions of being transported immediately to some mystical place where all your problems will be solved. It is probably true if you let your monkey mind, jumping all over the place, discourage you. The more your mind wanders, the better. This provides excellent exercise for your focus muscle bringing yourself repeatedly back to the breath (hundreds of times in a few minutes is quite normal).

Does this sound dreadfully boring to you? You wouldn't be normal if it didn't. This most basic type of meditation is quite difficult for beginners. But there are other meditation focuses that are much more accessible and just as useful.

Focus

THERE ARE MANY TYPES OF MEDITATION; THE ONLY difference among them is the object of focus. Here are a few I invite you to try.

Wide sky, ocean or nature focus, a mindfulness meditation

Sit yourself down in the middle of someplace you find beautiful or inspiring. The ocean is my favorite. Start by taking a few breaths, then pay attention to every sound, the salty smell, the white foamy waves hitting the shore, the sunlight as it is reflected by the ripples, the seaweed-covered rocks as they become covered by the incoming tide. You will be amazed by all that is going on around you when you pay attention. When your mind wanders, as it will, bring it back again and again. Just lose yourself in the wonder of this moment. Soon your ego will be napping in the sun. Your inner being may puff out a few insights, maybe not. That's cool when it happens, but it is NOT the goal. Sitting in the forest, in a garden, on the lawn looking up at the sky, the possibilities are endless. Relaxation is a likely lovely side effect, but not the goal.

Imagery

In this meditation your focus is images of your choosing. Just set an image in your mind. Perhaps you are picturing yourself in the forest or any place you find inspiring. Let your imagination go wild picturing every detail of this scene.

Walking through my imaginary forest, I see dappled light coming through the branches of the trees overhead. I see wildflowers poking through, randomly, unexpectedly, delighting me with their presence. I smell a rich pine scent as pine needles crunch beneath my feet. I see squirrels scurrying about fulfilling their squirrelness. Walking along, I come to a mountain stream that has formed the most delicious-looking pond that invites me in with the promise of cool repose away from the heat. Floating there, I am awash with gratitude for these precious moments of reverie.

Imagination is very much in the wheelhouse of inner being. The ego steps back in bewilderment and is knocked off balance by imagery. Suddenly, it doesn't have much to say.

Amid this dreamy reverie, you might want to take the next step. With the ego napping, the inner being is alert and waiting to impart information to you. Floating blissfully in my imaginary pond, I might ask questions about anything. Was there a purpose in this recent heart attack? What was the reason for interrupting my healthy swimming addiction when I have found it so healthy and life affirming?

Images of answers might fly right back at you, or you may get nothing. Just understand that asking the questions in this slightly altered level of consciousness is enough. Sooner or later the answers will come in one form or another. It's the asking that gives the inner being permission to start having more of an impact on your life.

Too woohoo for you? I can see my brother, who I love more than anything, recoiling in horror should he ever read this. It is not for everyone, but I ask you to remain open.

Lovingkindness meditation

THE FOCUS HERE IS TO MENTALLY SEND KIND AND loving wishes to everyone in your life. Using phrases like may you be well, may you be happy, may you be healthy, may you be filled with lovingkindness and may you be at peace is traditional, but just holding people in your hearts and sending them your love is fine.

This focus softens us and the more you do it, the more likely you will bring these things forward in your day-to-day life. Sending love to our family (most of them), friends and acquaintances is pretty easy. But doing it for people with whom you have conflict or worse is also part of the instruction, as is sending lovingkindness to yourself.

I was at a yoga retreat in my old hippyland of western Massachusetts when Donald Trump was elected president in 2016. When we came out of our rooms in the morning, we were all sobbing. Much of the day was used to process the grief and fear we were all feeling. My suggestion that we all send lovingkindness to the Donald was rejected even by the crunchiest granola types in attendance. But in Buddhist thought, only love has the power to change anything. For me, it was worth a try. It didn't change our president, but it changed me for the better; and that's the point.

This meditation softens your feelings toward everyone (including yourself). This is a crucial step in forgiveness of yourself and others.

Forgiveness is something you do for yourself. not for the other person. It allows you to move on with your story without the turmoil or hatred that may be attached to another's story. It is necessary for any sense of inner peace.

When we are unable to forgive, we remain angry, unhappy and tied to a story that brings us only pain and suffering. Forgiveness does not excuse another person's behavior. It does not mean that you need to keep him/her in your life. It simply means letting go of the hurt and moving along as best and as soon as you can.

The Buddha points out that there is only one reason someone else treats you badly, and that is his own suffering. This realization can soften you enough to have compassion for this enemy even if you cannot have him/her in your life. When I was working with people who were dying, it was clear that people who continue to be angry at themselves or others tend to have a much more difficult death. Forgiveness is a real gift for everyone.

Movement meditation

YOGA, TAI CHI AND WALKING MEDITATION ARE WHAT we generally think of as the movement meditations. In these practices, it's not only the movement but focusing on every sensation associated with the movement that makes them deeply satisfying and rewarding. By coaxing your mind to focus on this while letting other thoughts drift off into the ether somewhere, your ego starts going along for the ride rather than directing you unmercifully toward some more "practical" goal. Maintaining the focus is a challenge but be gentle with yourself as you acknowledge then let go of each thought intrusion. Your focus muscle will get stronger and stronger. Incredible relaxation is the reward, but, again, not the goal.

There is nothing mystical about yoga. Though magnificent on every level, it is not the only way to get there. Doesn't matter if you are walking, jogging, using an elliptical machine, rowing or swimming, deep focus on the detail of the activity is what makes the magic happen.

My two-hour-a-day swimming schedule is also my meditation time. Feeling every sensation, every breath, every muscle twinge, the coolness, the gliding sensation and on and on transforms this exercise into something truly amazing. On my best days, I literally feel swim drunk, akin, I suppose to being in the zone. Zone is a real phenomenon that comes from attending only to the experience of exercise itself.

And in two hours, you better believe everyone I have ever known is bathed in lovingkindness. I come out of that gym loving everyone. Wouldn't it be nice if we all felt that way more of the time? It could change the world.

Music meditation

THIS IS SOMETHING WE ALL HAVE DONE WHETHER we recognize it or not. Have you ever put on a pair of headphones and just let yourself dissolve into the haunting beauty of the music? This total immersion, savoring every sound, every lyric, every instrument, every voice, is transformative. As in moments of grace, the ego is soothed a bit, allowing the light it usually chases away to come in and transform a dark mood into a lighter one, a bad day into a better one. It is magic indeed, and something I suspect everyone can relate to.

But it is just music, how is it a meditation?

FOCUS, that's how.

Fearing I may have blown some minds with all this woohoo meditation talk, I will do something more scientific to bring you back into the fold. More meditation to come later, but here's your break.

Oops, can't leave the beach without collecting my ego. She is currently floating somewhere off the shore on a raft, sipping her rum punch. Better get her before she floats out to sea. I will need her for the next bit.

Physical effects of meditation

IF WAKING YOUR INNER BEING IS NOT ENOUGH FOR you, hundreds of studies have shown the health benefits of meditation. **Fifteen minutes a day of meditation reverses the effect of stress on your body for twenty-four hours**. Not a huge commitment, though here, more is definitely more.

You are probably all familiar with the stress response, the body's immediate reaction to perceived danger. In and of itself we could not survive without this stress response. We get into trouble when the stress response continues unabated as with anxiety or chronic worry. We do this much of the time, do we not?

Partial list of conditions either caused or exacerbated by stress

- **Musculoskeletal system** – Increased muscle tension leading to chronic headaches, migraines, chronic neck, back and upper extremity pain. Worrying about pain adds yet another layer of stress, making the pain more chronic and worse. Muscle atrophy due to disuse.

- **Respiratory system** – Shortness of breath, hyperventilation, airway constriction, exacerbation of asthma and COPD, panic attacks.

- **Cardiovascular system** – Increased heart rate, stronger heart muscle contraction, increased blood pressure, hypertension, heart attack, stroke, inflammation of coronary arteries, increased cholesterol levels.

- **Endocrine system** – Increased glucocorticoids (cortisol), which affects every cell in our bodies, not in a good way. Chronic fatigue, diabetes, obesity, depression and immune disorders, to name a few.

- **Gastrointestinal system** – damage to brain–gut communication triggering pain, bloating, gut discomfort, vomiting. Affects gut bacteria that can impact the ability to think and affect emotions and mood.

- **Esophagus** – Heartburn, reflux, esophageal spasm, difficulty swallowing, burping.

- **Bowel** – Pain, bloating, diarrhea, constipation, muscle spasms. Affects absorption and causes increased gas and weakened intestinal barrier, allowing gut bacteria to enter the body. Exacerbation of inflammatory bowel disease or irritable bowel syndrome. Increased gut nerve sensitivity.

- **Nervous system** – Signals adrenals to release adrenalin and cortisol responsible for cardiac, respiratory, digestive issues described above as well as wear and tear of the whole body.

- **Reproduction** – Males: decreased sex drive, impotence, decreased sperm production and motility. Females: irregular menstrual cycle, painful periods, changes in length of cycles, decreased sex drive, increased infertility. Affects postpartum adjustment, which can affect fetal and child-hood development and worsen PMS. Increased menopausal symptoms, hot flashes, anxiety, mood swings and feelings of distress. Exacerbation of herpes simplex virus, polycystic ovarian syndrome.

- **Aging** – Recent studies on aging and meditation show benefits relating to the specific needs of the elderly. Meditation increases focus, concentration, attention span, self-esteem, self-awareness, memory, sleep, strength, flexibility and balance. It decreases depression, pain, stress and anxiety. It boosts the immune system, fosters self-esteem, fights addiction. And lovingkindness meditation just makes grouchy old people nicer – truth. One doesn't even need to believe in it for things to improve (although it does help). Dedicating a minimum of fifteen minutes a day causes measurable change.

Again, these are all incredible side effects of meditation. Going into meditation, gritting your teeth, saying, "Go down, blood pressure, go down," will probably have the reverse effect. Drop the expectations of any particular outcome; just do it. Your inner being will take care of the rest. Woohoo!

Neurotransmitters, the Keys to the Kingdom

SO, FROM THE ABOVE DISCUSSION, IT IS VERY CLEAR how beneficial meditation is for the body, but it goes much deeper than that. All kinds of meditation activate feel good neurotransmitters that affect our bodies, minds, emotions and, if you will, our spirits. They are the keys that activate parts of our brain not generally accessed during our ego-driven lives.

Meditation, dancing, hugging, sex, music, exercise, prayer and being with friends are only a few of the things that cause surges in these amazing neurotransmitters. Here are the major players.

Oxytocin

Called the love chemical, oxytocin is best known for initiating uterine contractions, childbirth, lactation and bonding in a loving way with one's offspring. It surges when hugging, having sex, breastfeeding, playing with your baby or children or petting your animals. It is associated with great joy and feeling loved. It encourages social interaction, sexual arousal, building relationships, romance and engendering trust. It enhances growth and healing and decreases blood pressure and stress by decreasing cortisol. Oxytocin decreases pain, assists with sleep and encourages pro social behaviors and communication.

Oxytocin enables neuroplasticity, or the ability to change or build neural structure. When bathed in oxytocin, it is almost like the neural structures are fertilized, causing branches and new growth of the neural tissue. Altering our brain structure in this way makes us increasingly and permanently more sensitive to the effects of oxytocin. We become aware, on a cellular level, that we are all connected and that love is the only true answer to the world's problems. It helps us see our connection to something much bigger and more important than our selves.

Research has shown that psychedelic drugs in high doses provide a huge blast of oxytocin, resulting in the user's experience of pure love and God awareness. Very tiny doses have effects very similar to meditation. Thankfully, there are so many ways to activate oxytocin, we don't really need to all be on LSD, but it points to the fact that we really are mind, body and spirit by design.

Having said that, research is also showing that psychedelics, when used in controlled settings and micro dosing (1/10 the hallucinogenic dose), show great promise in treating PTSD, depression and suicidal ideation, and in easing the suffering of people who are dying. Used safely, these medications may assist in connecting to the spiritual, enhancing life's very meaning.

Serotonin

The other major feel-good neurotransmitter, serotonin, is crucial for learning, memory, sense of happiness, focus and calmness. It is necessary for sleep, wound healing and bone and sexual health. Usable levels of serotonin are markedly decreased in depression, anxiety, mania, digestive disorders, suicidal ideation, OCD, PTSD, panic disorder, schizophrenia and phobias.

Current medications for depression and the other disorders mentioned above are based on making more serotonin available to neuroreceptors by a variety of methods. They have been very helpful, but there are other more healthy and natural ways to get this increased serotonin effect.

Broken record aside, should I do the list again? Focused breathing, meditation, exercise, prayer, music, wild dancing and movement, yoga, contemplation, prayer, sex, hugging, mindfulness of your present moment, playing with your child, relationships and friends all do more than any medication can. The benefits go way further than our bodies.

Swim Drunk

LET'S LOOK AT A REAL-LIFE EXAMPLE OF HOW THIS all works. I mentioned previously my total sense of well-being during and after swimming. Just what is happening here? Muscles are oxygenated, making them healthy and highly functional. Joints are bathed in lubricating fluid, making them less painful both during and after swimming. A great cardio workout gives my heart and lungs their best shot at health and maximal function. Our bodies were built to move. When we do what our bodies need, we are rewarded with vibrant health and well-being. Total body movement also causes surges in both oxytocin and serotonin with all their effects.

We have all heard how exercise causes the release of endorphins (as do massage, eating, especially dark chocolate, sex). Endorphins help relieve pain, reduce stress and improve your sense of well-being. They are natural pain relievers and feel-good chemicals because they help you feel better and put you in a positive state of mind. They ease symptoms of depression, decrease stress and anxiety, improve self-image and contribute to weight loss.

Endurance in swimming requires focused, relaxed and rhythmic breathing. This action alone revs the body up with further blasts of oxytocin, serotonin and other feel-good substances. Focused breathing gathers all your thoughts and unconscious mind wanderings and brings them all inside yourself, where they can be experienced anew. This phenomenon is known as embodiment.

All those ego-driven thoughts, now gathered from all over the place to inside yourself, can be viewed with the much softer lens of love, connection, spiritual sensibility and way less fear than when viewed solely from the concrete and fearful ego, all because of the effects of oxytocin and serotonin.

Swimming is also the perfect time to meditate. Rhythmic breathing and the resulting embodiment brings all parts of us together such that meditation can do its best work. This puts your body/mind in the most receptive state for the benefits of meditation.

During my daily two-hour swim sessions, I have time for all the practices I mentioned. Starting always with mindfulness, I pay attention to every part of my body as it moves through the water. I focus on both how healthy and happy my joints feel. I also focus on areas that might be stressed and question why this might be happening. Sensing mild lower back pain, I question what I might do to make it better and what circumstances in my life might be making it worse. As more oxytocin and serotonin blasts away in my central nervous system I am more likely to understand the causes of this discomfort and do something about it.

Imagery can be used to send healing messages to these areas. After several minutes, the discomfort often just dissolves by doing nothing more than imagining it happening. Oxytocin and serotonin are surging even more, encouraging this healing to happen.

Lovingkindness, the meditation of sending loving messages to others in our lives, the good, the bad and the ugly, is very special. Oxytocin surges more here than any other meditation practice, thereby softening and enhancing feelings of love to those who are close to us while encouraging compassion and forgiveness for those with whom we have conflict. All the while, the oxytocin fertilized neurocircuitry grows making these positive changes permanent.

I mentioned earlier that I love everybody in the universe after a good, long, meditative swim. Who knew world peace, love and acceptance might come down to teaching the world how to access these amazing neurochemicals? It's mind-blowing if you really think about it.

With my brain now drenched in these incredible neurotransmitters, I am in the unique position of being able to look at conflicts or problems in my life through new lenses that make solutions more obvious. Using all parts of my brain rather than just the ego-dominated thought process makes life and all its problems easier.

Add to this listening to music with the use of underwater headphones. And bam! This is my brain on drugs! Good, natural drugs made from my own inner pharmacy. Swim drunk, this sense of total relaxation, well-being, love of all of humanity and how we are all connected can be accessed at will every day. Now THAT is amazing!

Your Life as a Meditation: Mindfulness

TO BE MINDFUL IS TO BE AWARE OF EVERY ASPECT of life, your feelings, your physical sensations, those around you, your environment and what you are doing in every moment. A celebration of the present moment is vital in life. To practice mindfully is to immerse yourself in whatever is happening moment to moment.

According to John Lennon, "Life is what is happening while you are making other plans."

Picture yourself at your child's wedding or some other event for which you have worked and planned for many months. Instead of being fully present in the joy of the moment, your mind (that damn ego again) is stressing. Are the decorations all right? Why did we seat Aunt Millie next to Aunt Marion when they hate each other? And God, that mother-in-law? How will our Suzie ever cope with that beast? Will anyone here stay to help me clean up? I have so much to do next week, how will I cope?

Our ego-controlled minds are always focusing on the mistakes or concerns of the past or anxieties about the future. The present moment (therefore our lives) is lost, never to return. It is such a tragedy to have missed the sheer beauty and wonder of the day, the gentle tears as the couple takes their vows, the love of those in attendance, the flowers, the music, the dancing, the speeches, the lovely food. Yet this is what we do, isn't it?

The ego is all about the past and the future. Gee, I wonder what is responsible for the present moment. You guessed it, our inner being. Placing ourselves smack dab into every detail of the present moment is a huge invitation for your inner wisdom to express itself. As I have said many times, this is where the action is.

In its simplest form, mindfulness meditation is a conscious effort to be present completely for what is presenting itself right here, right now. Start always with focusing on the breath (what could be more present than that), then on everything you are experiencing. The sights, sounds, smells, physical sensations, your emotions—everything, even your thoughts.

Wait a minute, aren't we supposed to acknowledge then dismiss intrusive thoughts? In many types of meditation, yes. But with mindfulness, thoughts are very much a part of this moment. So instead of dismissing your thoughts, look at and carefully examine them. Stay focused on them. What are they telling me? Is there something I can do about this situation or is it mindful acceptance that I need?

The point is to examine and stay focused on the concern at hand. Don't get carried away as our thoughts tend to bounce all over the place making mindfulness impossible. Just returning to the breath calms down all the noise.

Mindfulness in Health

THE BODY SCAN IS A TECHNIQUE WHERE WE FOCUS, in detail, on every sensation, ache, pain, sense of warmth and tension our body has right here and now. By attending this way we're telling our bodies, *Okay, I'm listening.* Generally, we go through life ignoring the headache, the hunger, the aches and pains that may be trying to get our attention to impart something of dire import to our lives.

So, as you are scanning every sensation from head to toe, inquire as to what these sensations may be telling you. *Okay, headache and sore muscles, why are you here?* Just breathe and be present for whatever messages you may get back. You may get blasted with images right away or you might get nothing. Trust the power of just asking the question. Trust that answers will come and understand that the pain might just go away having been recognized.

I had horrendous migraine headaches daily for years while working in the ER, raising kids and having a husband who couldn't be more different than me. During one particularly bad headache, I closed my eyes, breathed and then inquired about why these headaches were so bad and so omnipresent. My ego was saying, *You have a brain tumor, you are going to die, better get that MRI immediately* while my inner wisdom was saying, *Just settle down and pay attention.*

The images I got back were my husband's face and the face of my boss, the ER director. *What? How can this be? I love my husband and my job. They certainly are not responsible for causing this pain. Are they?*

On further inquiry, I realized it was not them specifically; it was more what I was doing to myself. Having never thought that I was as smart as my husband or as capable as my doctor colleagues, I tried to change myself to be more like them. Inner beings are very definite about our need and responsibility to be who we are, not to try to be someone else. You and your body will pay big time for such nonsense.

And you know what? The headaches, neck pain and sore muscles started to respond. I felt better as I finally accepted that the gifts I have as a doctor, though different in many ways, are just as valuable. Patch and I, fully united, have worked our own special magic in the healing of our patients. And no headaches. Now that's cool.

Inner Wisdom and the Heart Attack

MANY YEARS OF MEDITATING AND LIVING IN THE present moment much of the time has relegated my ego to an understudy role, being called only when necessary to drag me through the necessities of life. Inner wisdom is thankfully just a breath or two away.

The reason for the heart attack is clear—to remind me I am getting older and need to bow to that at least occasionally. My dear therapist, mother of my heart and cherished friend Barbara, would always give me a hug on parting and say, "Be gentle with yourself, my dear." Perhaps I have finally listened. It also inspired me to get this book written. Us old folks need to be reminded that as long as we are still alive, we need to live fully, genuinely.

Mindfulness in Parenting

CHILDREN NEED FOOD, CLOTHING, SHELTER, LOVE, safety, guidance—you know the list. It's straightforward. But as much as anything else, they benefit from our mindful attention.

I worried that my youngest daughter, Sarah, who required constant movement, activity and entertainment, would suffer when I needed to rest for several weeks after a hysterectomy. But instead of being traumatized, she loved just sitting with me every day, reading, having tomato soup with crackers and snuggling. Having my total undivided attention (the other kids being in school) obviated the need for us both to be running around crazily as was our habit. It was magic.

She also loved to be gently massaged every night (yeah, life was tough at my house). This helped a great deal, but only if I was mindfully focused on her. If my mind was elsewhere, as it often was, she would pick up on it immediately and say, "You're not doing it right." Kids just get it.

Children are the mindful geniuses of the world. Focusing on every detail of their play, attending to physical urges and sensations, they live only in the present moment. What a blessing to not be trapped by the disappointments of the past or the worries about the future. They expect and need the same thing in return.

Mindful Eating

WE MISS MUCH OF THE JOY IN EATING AS WE CRAM down fast food while driving, thinking and working. The glory of food gets lost in our crazy, multitasking existences. And what a shame this is. Food is one of the most wonderful gifts we have as human beings aside from being required for life itself. As elders, we really do have the time to just sit, chew and truly enjoy everything about the experience of eating. But do we do that? Generally, no.

Our egos have more important things to do than to savor the flavors, the sweetness, the rich experience of nourishing ourselves. Stuck in the past, or worrying about the future, we miss out on the wonder of this gift. This results in the mindless consumption of food that is not very good for us, is not pleasurable and has serious ramifications for our health and well-being.

Mindful eating practice, yet another meditation, is very simple. Sit yourself down, close your eyes, breathe and just get into every taste, every sensation of eating or drinking what is in front of you. Allow yourself to appreciate how amazing it is to sense the coolness of a piece of fresh pineapple, the sweetness, the juice blasting through your mouth with every bite, the odd but interesting bite it leaves on your tongue. Food eaten mindfully is much more satisfying. You tend to eat a lot less. And as you pay attention to your body as it is going down, you can't help but make better food choices for yourself. Yet another win-win.

Mundane Task Meditation

YOU KNOW HOW WASHING DISHES OR PICKING UP the kitchen for the umpteenth time can be annoying when there are better things you could be doing? Same goes for all the tasks we routinely do just to keep our homes and life together. Yes, even these can be meditations. Focus on the details of washing the dishes. Feel the warm water. Appreciate the texture and smell of the white suds. Observe the food and grease being wiped off revealing the perfect, smooth shine on your dishes. Paying attention in this way makes even the most mundane, boring task oddly satisfying as it relaxes you.

Discovering you are almost out of gas as you are hurrying to get somewhere can totally wreck a small portion of your day. Instead of ranting, raving and swearing at yourself, accept your situation, open the door, attend to all the credit card stuff and feel the gas pumping into the tank. Close your eyes, breathe, feel the cool air, the faint fumes from the gas and appreciate that the world has made you slow down a bit.

The Healing Nature of Everything

IT WOULD BE IMPOSSIBLE TO HAVE GOTTEN THIS FAR in the book and not realize EVERYTHING can be a meditation. Phobic about fast rides and roller coasters, I was uncertain how I would take my youngest daughter, Sarah, on all the rides she would certainly not want to miss during our mother-daughter trip to Disney World. Reaching into my meditation goody grab bag, I would approach this fear mindfully. With a few deep breaths, instead of screaming and wishing God would just take me, right then, right there, I started paying attention to every detail of that ride. I focused on the twists, turns, speed and physical sensations as I continued to breathe. This resulted in the sensation that, fully present, fear disappeared, making this and the twenty-six subsequent rides on Space Mountain quite delightful. Try this at the dentist. It works. Try it every time you are frightened or frustrated. It changes your perception of everything.

Mindfulness and Acceptance

AHH, HOW LOVELY IT IS TO SIT MINDFULLY ON A beach, eat amazing food, spend very loving and mindful times with our children. Life affirming in every way. But mindfulness is not all joy, happiness and light.

To be truly mindful we must also be willing to sit with the difficult things in our lives. During my husband's stroke and the thirteen-year (and counting) aftermath, certain realities had and still must be faced. There is no running away. The attempt to do so will guarantee an increase in my physical symptoms and dash any hope of peace.

So, if your present moment is filled with fear, worry, a sense of loss of control, just be with it. Stay in that dark place as long as you need to and breathe. The last thing you need right now is to have your ego yammering away at you about what should be done or how you should feel. Allow your inner wisdom to help you look at the situation with the lenses of patience, compassion and respect for everything you are going through. Over time, this will help you accept this reality and make peace with it. Pushing pain away always makes it worse.

Driving back and forth through six months of my husband's hospitalization and rehab, I found myself saying repeatedly, *I am okay in this moment. Oh, and I am okay in this moment, and in this moment.* No matter what was happening, I could tolerate just one moment at a time. We can always tolerate the present moment—always. But at the end of the day, I wondered how every moment of the day was okay and yet my life still sucked! That is the work of the vicious ego, judging, being impatient and just wanting this to all go away. In times of great turmoil, one day (or one moment) at a time is how we survive. And so be it.

Mindfulness and Attachment

IN BUDDHIST THOUGHT, WE SUFFER NOT BECAUSE of the things that happen to us but because we are so attached to things being different. In our society, we are set up for this disappointment as we have been taught having everything we want in our lives is a birthright. It is not. By witnessing our lives quietly, the good and the bad, the beautiful and the ugly, the joyful and the sad, in the presence of our inner wisdom, we practice letting go of attachments that don't serve us.

Suffering is a part of life, so even our judgment that suffering is a bad thing must be suspended. It just is. Our lives are made up of all extremes, good and bad, darkness and light, well-being and pain, success and failure. Being mindful requires peaceful acceptance of it all. The ego can't help us here. Our inner wisdom can.

Back to Aging

AS WE BACK AWAY FROM MANY OF THE THINGS THAT consumed our lives when younger, we have a beautiful opportunity to just be here now. We have so much to learn about ourselves and who we really are. The beauty of the world, our friends and family and the grace that is all around us is there for the asking. Just breathe, whenever you can, and take it all in. What a gift.

Gratitude

MULTIPLE VERY SOLID STUDIES HAVE SHOWN THAT feeling grateful for all you have been given is one of the best things you can do for your own health and well-being. Customarily thought of as something you do for someone else, saying thank you is just the right thing to do. But it is so much more than that.

Studies show that even something as simple as writing down ten things for which you are grateful every day, like meditation, diminishes the physical sequelae of stress. I know you now know what's coming next. Focusing on gratitude, whether in writing or meditation, brings my inner being energetically to the fore. She instructs every cell in my body to function to its maximum capacity and makes my heart sing!

So, sitting here once again at the beach, I am grateful for the incredible peace I feel here. The tiny waves are a mere trickle as they come to rest on the sun-warmed sand. Listening to the beautiful piano music I have chosen to accompany me on my writing journey today, how could I not be grateful? The warmth of the sun is perfectly balanced by the cool sea breeze. Is it possible that heaven is better than this? I can't imagine it.

Closing my eyes, I see the beautiful faces of my children and my little grandson, JoJo. I picture the friends with whom I will be spending a glorious girls' retreat next week on the Connecticut shore.

My Dunkin Donuts iced coffee has never tasted better, yet another gift. I could go on like this for hours and often do. My gratitude has gifted me with an equanimity and peace that is truly life affirming as it can be for you.

A Most Mindful Hobby: Photography

UNTIL RECENTLY, I COULDN'T TAKE A GOOD PICTURE if my life depended on it. Photos not mindfully taken of a building, a monument or even the beautiful ocean were bland and colorless.

Everything changed during my trip to Vietnam and Bali several years ago. As a result of my age and hippiness, the memories of the Vietnam War hit me on the deepest level. I needed to float on a sampan along the Mekong Delta. I needed to feel the extreme heat and humidity of the jungles. I needed to feel the sweat and terror our servicemen felt as they dragged themselves through the oppressive rain forest. I needed to visit the devastating American war museum that verified all the horror I always felt deep down inside.

As deeply disturbing things tend to do, walls cracked and fell. With my inner being now bathed in light, I was graced once again with knowing that beauty and terror coexist in this world. It was the extreme sadness and horror that cracked me open enough to see beauty in an entirely different way.

Focusing now more on emotion than just taking a picture, everything was suddenly so colorful, so heartbreakingly beautiful, that my little iPhone camera and I vowed that it is beauty and emotion that needed to be captured, not just the sights.

The colors of the culture were so vibrant. Women glowed in their magnificent saris as they brought gifts of thanks to the temples. As flowers thrived in the heat and humidity, they welcomed being remembered for all time even on my little camera.

Floating in a pool in Bali, with camera in hand, I learned seeing things from all angles made the most impressive shots. Drifting slowly under a huge flowering shrub with branches gracefully draped overhead, I appreciated the flowers more when seeing from beneath with the sun and sky peeking through. Seeing things from all angles is pretty cool, no matter what you are doing. So, I now take amazing photos, if I do say so myself. Finding the humanity, soul, emotion and color wherever I go makes photography one of the most mindful things I can do. Yet another meditation of pure joy.

Miss Rumphius

THIS REMARKABLE BOOK, GIVEN TO MY CHILDREN from my dear friend Beth before she passed, tells the story of Little Alice. Enthralled by all the tales of worldwide travel and adventure her grandfather conveyed to her as she sat, daily, on his lap, she planned her own future of seeing the world and everything in it. As Alice and her grandfather walked on the beach right in front of his little cottage, she decided she must live by the sea. Her granddad thought this sounded lovely, but he said there was one more thing she must do. She must do something to make the world a more beautiful place.

So, Alice traveled all over the world. She broadened her horizons by spending precious time meeting and appreciating everyone she met. Entering late middle age, she decided it was time to finally settle in her home by the sea. She planted lovely flowers all around and made it her forever home. After living there happily for many years, she slipped into old age, as we all do. Now bedbound due to an illness, she felt great sadness about not having fulfilled her grandfather's final wish.

Upon awakening one morning, she felt a little better. Gazing out her bedroom window, she was overcome by the rich beauty and vibrant color of the lupines planted so many years ago. Inspired, she finally realized what she needed to do.

Gently raising herself from her bed, she found her dusty old gardener's catalogue and bought three bushels of lupine seeds. Now known as the lupine lady, Miss Rumphius (formerly little Alice) would walk day by day, broadcasting the seeds up hill and dale, along the roadside, throughout empty fields—everywhere! People smiled politely, thinking this eccentric old lady had finally lost it.

As it took a few years for the lupines to establish themselves, Miss Rumphius passed away before seeing the full impact of her work. But her little beachside village, now blanketed each spring and summer in colorful bliss, became a symbol of the difference one little person can make.

So, as we get older, we might ask, "What have I done to make the world a more beautiful, better place?" As long as we are still alive, this is an opportunity we shouldn't miss. We are still capable of delivering beauty until our last breath leaves our bodies.

Making the world a more beautiful place can be very simple. Random acts of kindness as simple as buying a coffee for the person in line behind you at the Dunkin Donuts drive-up, helping a new mother as she struggles with baby, car seat and groceries, picking up a neighbor's trash barrel after the wind has blown it into the middle of the street. No big deal? I beg to differ.

I personally enjoy straightening out all the shopping carts left willy-nilly over grocery store parking lots, especially in the rain. A little crazy? I'm totally at peace with that kind of crazy. Something as simple as making eye contact with a gentle smile on your face while thanking a gas station attendant or store clerk and seeing that returned is life affirming for both.

When everyone matters, everything changes.

My work as a hospice medical director gifted me with meeting the most kind, loving, caring people one could imagine. People working with others as they make their transition from this world to the next take doing something beautiful for the world to a new level.

I especially treasured one kind, elderly volunteer who spent all day, every day, crocheting handmade teddy bears for every hospice patient. My husband just received a hand-crocheted angel from a volunteer in the facility he now requires. Does this make the world a more beautiful place? You bet it does.

My Buddha Boy

MY SON MIKE WILL BE HORRIFIED WHEN HE SEES this in print, but it must be said. Arriving from South Korea at five months, he sat contentedly with his big Buddha belly and a serene smile on his face. This is just who he is. He has always had a presence, so peaceful and welcoming that people can't help but love him. A very quiet, shy, solitary guy even to this day, his quiet equanimity continues to attract people. He has no idea whatsoever of his effect on the world. (And he will be blushing wildly when he sees this.)

The money I made from doing my lecture series over the years was all donated to charity, my favorite being the SEVA foundation. Started by one of my favorite gurus, Ram Dass, SEVA dedicated itself to curing blindness in the world. Each donation of $40 provided the means for one person to get cataract surgery, restoring sight to thousands worldwide.

Hearing about this, my then twelve-year-old son walked down quietly on Christmas morning and handed me a check for $800 payable to SEVA. He thought 20 percent of his current net worth of $4,000 was reasonable. He was also a hard worker and saver. On that Christmas morning, the peaceful smile on his face showed me that restoring sight to twenty people was his best Christmas gift. Now he is the kind of man who values contentment over happiness. He just gets it. He always has.

JoJo Jellybean

NO BOOK ON THE JOY OF AGING WOULD BE COM-
plete without a brief mention of our grandchildren. JoJo entered and
changed my world three and a half years ago. His face, his joy, his
constant smile and knowing looks grace me daily as FaceTime chats
keep us connected even though he lives across the country. These little
beings thrive on the love of their families, including their grandparents.
The deeper the bench of love, the better.

Grandparents have the special privilege of doing all the fun stuff
as parents must slog, as we all did, through the necessities and rules
of childrearing. There is no gift more fulfilling for both you and your
grandchild than to sit snuggled on the couch, read books or just be
totally and mindfully present to this little human. It is an amazing gift
to be given right up to your dying breath.

Weeds, What Weeds?

AS I BEGIN MY DISCUSSION OF RELIGION AND SPIR-
ituality, I do so with the perhaps unrealistic intention of not upsetting
anyone. Having taken on impossible tasks before, I recognize this is a
big one, and I promise to do my best. Why put myself through this?
Because it is important, that's why.

Why are we here? Does our life have purpose? What does it
all mean? Where do we go when we die? These questions become
more and more important as our time on this planet shortens. Who
is God? Is he a human-appearing spiritual being who, from his home
in heaven, has clear plans for our salvation? Do we live in some spir-
itually ordered cosmic universe that guides us during our lives to be
the best we can be? Is God present in every one of us (I like this idea)
present as a soul, the source of inner wisdom or Buddha nature? I
can't say for sure; nobody can.

Religion gives its followers a sense of certainty in this regard.
That in and of itself is kind of a wonderful thing when you think about
it. Although not a member of any organized religion, I do see their
value. As a young teenager I would sit quietly in our town's beautiful
Catholic church and bathe myself in the mystery, peace and quiet. Still
smelling the incense used during the last mass or hearing the organist
practice her hymns or watching a true devotee as he or she prayed

and lit candles in the glory of her Lord touched me deeply. My family wasn't even Catholic, for God's sake! Yet it comforted me on so many levels. No one could possibly have guessed what a little weirdo I was back then, unless you have read this book. It is now perfectly clear.

Needless to say, this odd little preteen girl piqued the interest of the nuns and priests. They graciously accepted me into the fold. And, since I was just being a kid, they all nurtured me in ways I would be hard-pressed to describe. I started going to mass every morning before school (this will be shocking to my old friends as they read it). I was confirmed into the Catholic Church when I was thirteen and remained a devoted believer until I entered the more grown-up world.

When I was eighteen, my eyes were opened to different people, races, viewpoints and religions. I will never forget the afternoon I spent talking to a seventy-three-year-old transvestite man in Provincetown. Such a sweet being just trying to be himself. At the time, these people would not have been welcomed by the Catholic Church. My search for spirituality would need to take a very different course.

What I still love about religions to this day are the ideas and values they share, not the doctrines that that divide them. Learning to love one's enemies, turning the other cheek and being present and generous to those who may need our help—these are the things around which I can vigorously wrap my arms. Whether you believe in Jesus as the son of God or not, you must admit, he was a pretty cool guy. Preaching love and peace, he is without a doubt the favorite of my hippy brethren.

We start getting caught up in the weeds when we hate each other for the god we choose to worship or for the beliefs that divide rather than join us. My comfort with Buddhist philosophy is that it claims no particular god. The Buddha himself would have been appalled if anyone thought of him as God. He was just an enlightened person who saw the struggle in our lives and proposed a way of gently and peacefully navigating it. He knew that what we need is a way to access what's inside to bring our best selves forward in the service of humanity.

Simply stated, religions are at their greatest when they lead us to be the best and kindest human beings possible. By greeting everyone with a Namaste, we vow to see their true loving nature rather than any of the darker aspects of their personalities, which we all have.

As for eternity, who knows for certain what this means? I kind of like the idea that consciousness continues in a bodiless plane unimaginable to the human psyche. But I remain open to an all-loving God, peace, angels and seeing those who went before me.

This is not something we should be fighting or having wars over. But for people entering the later stages of life, having a personal spirituality that gives you peace and equanimity no matter what the future may hold is a precious thing indeed.

Yin/Yang, the Sand Dollar, the Lotus and the Butterfly

SIMPLE OBJECTS SUCH AS THESE HAVE BEEN assigned special spiritual characteristics that help us clarify what is important in life. Some of these symbols are well known and appreciated around the world. Others, placed on earth especially for you, may come to you unbidden.

Just Remember This

The principle of Yin/Yang depicted by this symbol is that all things exist as inseparable and contradictory opposites. Without darkness, you cannot have light. Looking at the image, you will see that within darkness, there is always a little light (hope). Within light, there is always a little darkness (fear that the light will end). Like a lava lamp, these areas increase and decrease, melding into one another. This movement is constant, showing that all experience is impermanent.

Meditation and all the other practices mentioned above will not change this reality. The circle can never turn white.

The Buddha taught meditation to decrease suffering, not to change this reality. By inviting one's inner being to participate, the blows of the darkness are softened. The small light of hope shines ever brighter. We learn to accept the truth of impermanence. The recognition that good times can't last and that bad times will surely come again doesn't devastate us quite so much. Our inner beings, accessed through meditation, guide us to a more peaceful acceptance of things just as they are. Now, that is some gift!

Sand Dollar

Walking along the beach many years ago during a time of personal turmoil, I happened upon a sand dollar. A sand dollar is a work of art. What makes it so? Presenting a beautiful flower-like pattern with a solid center from which symmetric and balanced petals emanate, one petal is no more important than the rest. All merge into an awe-inspiring pattern. Is this not true with people, the most serene of whom being those who are themselves centered, whose lives are similarly balanced? Work no more important than family, one plan or desire not more important than the next, one child equally as important as the others? A representation of all we are in our lives, the sand dollar brings us back, over and over, to finding a way to put it all in balance.

Underlying the prominent flower design is a subtle mosaic, representing perhaps our talents, skills, dreams, heretofore not recognized by ourselves or others. One of the tasks throughout our lives is to develop these less obviously seen parts of our being, to invite them to become an equal petal in the design.

Looking carefully on the sand dollar's surface, you will also find delicate lines emanating from the center, through the middle of each petal, and extending to the periphery of the shell. It is a message, perhaps, that everything we hold dear must also extend from our being to the outside world. The world benefits as we share the most important parts of ourselves.

On the sand dollars under surface is a tiny hole. Peering inside, from this limited perspective, is an intricate network of shell-like structural foundation. Deeply embedded and mostly not visible to the human eye, one can only ponder what lies beneath. Much like our human essence, it defies superficial perusal.

Is this not like the inner wisdom or Buddha nature of which I speak voluminously? It takes much work, introspection and perhaps even breaking open a bit to allow enough light to enter to even begin to gain an understanding of what this is all about. This goes for sand dollars and ourselves in equal proportion.

If you shake a sand dollar's shell, you may hear something solid bouncing around inside. These are five teeth that have become detached over time. When the shell of the sand dollar is split open, these five loose teeth look exactly like doves! Make of this what you will. Messages like this abound if you can be open to them. Symbols of meaning are ours for the asking.

The Lotus

Appreciated in many cultures as a symbol of the reality of life itself, the lotus helps us understand the enormous value of the darker side of our lives. Looking at this beautiful blossom as it floats serenely and magnificently on the ponds surface, we may not understand that it is rooted in the most God-awful muck. Yet it still manages to rise, phoenix-like, un-battered and beautiful despite its origins.

The lotus invites humans to consider it very seriously. Whether one had an unhappy childhood, a bad marriage, a terrible diagnosis or just all the "shit" that mires us into the feeling that our lives just suck, the lotus asks us to reconsider our perspective. It is without a doubt all the muck in our lives that provides the fertilizer we so need to be the best and most beautiful being we can be, just like the lotus.

The Butterfly

We all comprehend the symbolism of the butterfly. Moving from cocoon to butterfly can be likened to all the transformations that take place as we enter the various, all impermanent, changes in our lives. In our cocoon phases, we work, we slog through, we try to figure out what our next move will be, must be. Then, one day, the cocoon bursts open, allowing all we have worked so hard for, all we have suffered for, to burst forth in its supreme radiance. I look at med school graduation this way. The butterfly's life span is relatively short, but its presence is breathtaking for as long as it lasts. The butterfly, in its ultimate symbolic role, is perhaps best known for the radiant transition from this cocoon life to the next, which brings me to Lynn's legacy.

Lynn's Legacy

LYNN WAS MY BEST FRIEND, A SOULMATE ABOUT
everything that matters in life. She was diagnosed with ovarian cancer in her late thirties, causing devastation and enormous sadness to
everyone who knew her, especially me.

Western medicine, as good as it was, failed her. Years of che-
motherapy, baldness and sickness did not result in cure, just more
suffering. One day, she took my hand and said, "Chris, we are going
to do this journey together." And we did. To tell you that this was the
journey of my life is not hyperbole.

As devastating as this was, Lynn and I were both broken into
little pieces. The sadness prevailed. How could it not? But our bro-
kenness allowed the light to come in. And what a bright and radiant
light it was! Our daily talks reached so deeply into our very cores
that we rejoiced as each spiritual insight entered our consciousness.
In time she would say this death and dying business was not all bad
as it taught her and me so much about the meaning of our existence
on this planet.

We cried, we talked and, yes, we even laughed about the insanity of the lives we had been given. Lynn was by no means a religious
person. An unsuspecting hospice chaplain was doing her best to con-
vince Lynn to accept Jesus as her savior. She was appalled when Lynn

made it clear to me that the chaplain needed to leave. Forcing one's own religious beliefs onto another, especially one who is dying, is a special kind of violence.

Once the chaplain made her gently enforced exit, Lynn and I went into spasms of laughter. This was not as sacrilegious as it may seem, as we both have enormous respect for the messenger that Jesus was. He was possibly the world's best teacher about what was truly moral, loving and right.

As she closed her eyes she said dreamily, "Fabio, Fabio," recollecting that dreamboat of a model with long, Jesus-like hair. Her sense of humor is unmatched by anyone even now, twenty years later.

Day after day, we sat, we laughed, we tasted gumdrops and fried rice. We were as present to one another as any two people can be. It was among the best gifts either of us had ever been given.

Then, fully accepting her impending fate, Lynn decided it was time to work on her memorial service. She wanted me to do her eulogy as she didn't want to return to the dust without giving herself a fitting sendoff.

I wrote down a few notes and stories, but this eulogy needed Lynn herself. Using a gentle imagery meditation, she was brought to that inner being place where she could speak of what mattered to everyone she loved and to all who would be attending.

This Is Her Eternal Message

AS HUMAN BEINGS, WE SOMEHOW FEEL THAT WE
are our physical bodies, that it is the physical that makes us invincible,
when in fact our invincibility is deep inside where no one else can see.

She asks us to open ourselves up to all the love that is out there
for us and not to be afraid to ask for help.

> Believe in your inner voice and allow it to guide you
> through your life.
> Strive for the truth, which is always less frightening than
> the unknown.
> Realize everything you need is right there beside you.
> All you have to do is look and you will find it; it is closer
> than you can imagine.
> Don't let a disease become who you are, only something
> you must deal with and learn from.
> Work to keep anger away from your life.
> Never settle for what's clearly inequitable—you deserve
> better than that.
> Find happiness in simple things.

Ahhhh, my Lynn.

Lynn was very interested in how she would contact me and her other loved ones once she passed to the other side. Again, with gales of laughter, she would talk of flickering my lights, ringing my doorbell, stroking my cheek, hoping I might be able to feel some gentle warmth or vibration telling as me she was there. She admitted she didn't have any real idea what she would do (how could she), but she guaranteed it would be sweet. And it was.

Messages from Beyond

THE MORNING AFTER LYNN PASSED, I WENT TO THE beach. I was contemplating her memorial service that would take place a month later. She wanted Eva Cassidy's version of *Fields of Gold* to be played at the beginning of her service. I had asked her what other music she might like, and she just said I would know. Typical Lynn, I figured she was now looking down at me, snickering, as I struggled to figure this out.

Seeking inspiration, I put Eva Cassidy's *Songbird* CD into my player. *Fields of Gold*, the first cut on the album, just wouldn't come on. I tried over and over again, turning the player on and off, and still, it wouldn't play. It kept skipping to the fifth song on the album, *Songbird*. I thought it wise to listen. The lyrics stopped me in my tracks. Paraphrasing her hauntingly beautiful rendition of *Songbird* she sings, there's no need to keep crying, the sun will continue to shine, I will always be with you and I love you more than ever. She recorded this in January 1996 and passed away from melanoma in November of the same year. Now, 26 years later, Eva still brings sunshine and love into our lives...so does Lynn.

Gob-smacked, I now knew what other music needed to be played. So now bopping down the beach, sure Lynn had sent me her first message from the beyond, I thought it would be cool if she would send a butterfly to land on my shoulder while giving her eulogy. That would be a nice touch, far too dramatic for the likes of Lynn. But in this moment, I was truly giddy.

I got into my car and headed home. As I drove down the street, a small light-yellow butterfly with a black spot on each wing landed on my windshield wiper. It stayed there for the remaining five miles to my house. When I gently reached my hand out once I was home, this little being lighted gently on my hand for a moment then flew into the ether

Nahhhh, I thought to myself, *this cannot be, can it?* A few days later, I was out cleaning my winter-dirty pool. While I was vacuuming, an almost-black butterfly with bright orange markings landed on my hand. As I continued vacuuming for another fifteen minutes or so, it moved to my thigh. This butterfly was my steady companion. Hearing the doorbell ring, I took my little friend into the house. My visitor (having already heard the first butterfly story) gasped as this creature also disappeared into the ether. At that moment, I was filled with Lynn's scent, something with which I had become very familiar over the past several months.

And yet there is more, so much more. A few days later, I was drawn out my front door where a tiger swallow tail circled, hitting my door lightly with each rotation. I walked slowly to the middle of my front yard. Placing my hand gently on the ground, it landed ever so softly, leaving in a hurry when my golden retriever came to investigate. Lynn wasn't a fan of dogs, so this made me laugh.

Lynn felt I was wasting my life working in an ER. She felt I had the skills that could make my impact as a doctor much more valuable. One day she said, "My being sick and dying will have been worthwhile if you do something to change medicine." Jeez, no pressure there, Lynn, you little bugger.

Over the next year, I wrote and prepared my lecture series in mind–body medicine, teaching many of the concepts I have described in this book. Feeling quite frightened about presenting my very first lecture, I said out loud, "God damn it, Lynn, where are your damn butterflies now?" The world in 2002 was not ready to accept these "woohoo" teachings. Mindfulness and meditation were not by any stretch mainstream as they are now, just another nail in the coffin of my weirdness as a physician.

Well, as Lynn would have it, my doorbell rang a few hours before my lecture. It was her husband, Gerry, giving me a token earned celebrating his first year of sobriety. And you now know what it had on it—a butterfly, of course.

Right after my first lecture on spirituality in medicine, Marge, Lynn's dear hospice nurse, came up to me and said there was absolutely no doubt in her mind this was Lynn. Apparently, Lynn told Marge her plan to return as a bird—no, a butterfly—to comfort her family and friends.

Digging up ceramic butterflies in gardens, having butterflies or large moths wait patiently at my door, greeting me, then tearing about my house and back into the ether, are common experiences. My bed-bound husband, very left brained by nature, seeing this, would just say, "Hello, Lynn."

What Does This All Mean?

OF COURSE, THIS IS SUBJECT TO EVERYONE'S INDI-vidual interpretation. I don't expect anyone to drop their beliefs and values and rocket out to the far reaches of the cosmic universe, as I have. My only wish here is that perhaps even death can be looked at with different lenses. Learning to accept the certainty of our deaths, the worst of our nightmares, might be a very important part of living the rest of our days with joy and freedom. This is Lynn's legacy.

The Joy of Eldering

Leaving behind my journey of struggling and racing
through the white water of many rivers, I become
the river, creating my own unique way.

Leaving behind my self-imposed role as a tree upon which
others have leaned, I now become the wind, with the
freedom to blow whenever and wherever I choose.

Leaving behind the years of yearning for others to see
me as somebody, I soften into becoming my future,
with permission from SELF to continually unfold as I
choose, without concern for how others may see me.

Leaving behind the urge to provide answers for others, I become-in the silence of this forest retreat-
the question.

Leaving behind the rigor of my intellect, I become a single
candle in the darkness, offering myself as a beacon
for others to create their own path.

I became an elder.

By Cathy Carmody

UNCHAINED FROM THE MANY RESPONSIBILITIES I
took on throughout my life, I have this incredible opportunity to
become who I truly am. No longer needing ego to run the entire show

of my life, I am free to just be, to love unconditionally, to bask in the incredible beauty of this world and the gift of my life.

Wisdom, the gift we are given after living many years, is a gift we can share freely with younger souls on their own journeys. Now, having all the time in the world, we can really dig deep into the mystery of our inner being and discover who we really are, have always been and will always be.

As our life on earth gets closer to its end, we have the time and motivation to look deep inside ourselves to understand that what is coming may not be an ending after all. That perhaps this life is only one step of an endless journey of consciousness, impossible to comprehend by our limited human existence. And, finally, we can comprehend that love, not hate, generosity, not greed, connection, not isolation is the only way to create heaven on earth.

This is true joy.

This is real freedom.

This is the gift and promise of aging, ours for the asking.

This is my legacy.

Mama J Unchained is about living your best life, every day, espe[...] not denying the inevitable losses that come with aging, includin[...] turns traditional views of aging on their heads as they generally ne[...] in this part of our lives. Unchained from the stressful obligations o[...] are free to explore who we really are. Beneath our ego driven ne[...] raising children, keeping up appearances and making money lies [...] always been there but ignored in the pursuit of worldly goals. Call it [...] or Buddha nature, this part of us is always at peace, naturally lovin[...] wise and accepting of yourself and your life just as it is. Learning to view our lives through these lenses changes everything, perhaps making our last chapters the best ones yet.

DR. CHRISTA JOHNSON is a mother, retired family practice/ hospice physician, lecturer in Mind Body Medicine, author of Lynn's Legacy; Mind Body and Spirit (c2004). Prior to her medical career, she was a psychiatric social worker.

"I love, love, love, this book! Its refreshingly brief entries are little gems, like a diamond's facet each one bursts forth with reflected light. It provides wise and compassionate counsel without proselytizing or preaching. I hope it finds its way into many hands."

- Margaret (Peg) Baim, Benson-Henry Institute for Mind Body Medicine, Massachusetts General Hospital

"Equal parts wisdom, wit, and truth-telling, Mama J Unchained is a paradigm shifting guide to designing the best possible version of the rest of your life. Wherever you are on the aging trajectory, Dr. Johnson asks the important questions that will forever change the way we think about aging."

- Laurie O'Neil, MSW, co-author of Graceful Woman Warrior; A Story of Mindfully Living in the Face of Dying.

"This is not a book on aging; this is a prophetic book on living. It should be read by everyone who will eventually grow old. It is not a book about being happy in life but about the possibility of being mindful in all we do even when life hits us hard."

- Eliud Herrera Jr., student at the Gordon-Conwell Theological Seminary

A compelling, multifaceted read. It touched me and inspired me to approach life with reflection and appreciation. I loved it."

- Lawrence Todesca, Retired sales executive for a global, Fortune 50 technology firm.

"Having had the privilege of working with Dr. J in her role as Hospice Medical Director, it was a joy to read about the many facets and personal philosophies of 'her life journey' - put forth so humbly and eloquently in this sharing. A great read."

- Paul Methot, BSN - Hospice and Palliative Care RN

"Christa is truly an inspiration! She teaches us through humor and her life experiences that getting older is an adventure not to be missed."

- Attorney Sharon Hague

ISBN: 978-1-66789-488-1

9 781667 894881

WHAT AM I DOING HERE?

A Bewildered American in Britain

Kathy Flake